Beyond the School Gat

D0282264

Around the world, schools are being asked to offer new services to students, families and communities in order to overcome the effects of disadvantage.

Referred to as 'extended', 'full service' or 'community' schools, they extend their provision so that they are open beyond the normal school day, in order to work with families and local communities.

This book, for the first time ever, critically examines the role of full service and extended schools. The authors draw on their extensive international evaluations of this radical new phenomenon to ask:

- What do extended or full service schools hope to achieve, and why should services based on schools be any more effective than services operating from other community bases?
- What pattern of services and activities is most effective?
- What does extended schooling mean for children and families who are not highly disadvantaged, or for schools outside the most disadvantaged areas?
- How can schools lead extended services at the same time as doing their 'day job' of teaching children?
- Why should schools be concerned with family and community issues?
- Beyond the advocacy of 'extended provision', what real evidence is there that schools of this kind make a difference, and how can school leaders evaluate the impact of their work?

This book will be of interest to anyone involved in extended and full service school provision, as a practitioner, policy maker or researcher.

Colleen Cummings is a Research Associate in the Research Centre for Learning and Teaching, University of Newcastle, UK.

Alan Dyson is Professor of Education in the University of Manchester, UK, where he co-directs the Centre for Equity in Education. He was previously Director of the Special Needs Research Centre at the University of Newcastle.

Liz Todd is Professor of Educational Inclusion at the University of Newcastle. Her Routledge book, *Partnerships for Inclusive Education*, was shortlisted for the 2007 NASEN/TES Academic Book Award.

Beyond the School Gates

Can full service and extended schools overcome disadvantage?

Colleen Cummings, Alan Dyson and Liz Todd

Routledge
Taylor & Francis Group

LONDON AND NEW YORK

First published 2011
by Routledge
2 Park Square, Milton Park, Abingdon, Oxon, OX14 4RN

Simultaneously published in the USA and Canada
by Routledge
711 Third Avenue, New York, NY 10017

Routledge is an imprint of the Taylor & Francis Group, an informa business

© 2011 Colleen Cummings, Alan Dyson and Liz Todd

Typeset in Garamond & Gill Sans by Swales & Willis Ltd, Exeter, Devon

British Library Cataloguing in Publication Data
A catalogue record for this book is available from the British Library

Library of Congress Cataloging-in-Publication Data
Cummings, Colleen.
  Beyond the school gates : questioning the extended schools and
  full service agendas / Colleen Cummings, Alan Dyson and Liz Todd.
  p. cm.
  Includes bibliographical references and index.
  1. Children with social disabilities—Education—Great Britain.
  2. Children with social disabilities—Services for—Great Britain.
  3. Community and school—Great Britain.
  I. Dyson, Alan. II. Todd, Liz. III. Title.
  LC4096.G7C86 2011
  371.030941—dc22
  2010039707

ISBN: 978-0-415-54866-3 (hbk)
ISBN: 978-0-415-54875-5 (pbk)
ISBN: 978-0-203-82870-0 (ebk)

Contents

Acknowledgements

This book draws on research carried out over a number of years and involving various teams of researchers. We are particularly indebted to them for their work. They include Deanne Crowther, Ian Hall, Lisa Jones, Karen Laing, Daniel Muijs, Ivy Papps, Diana Pearson, Carlo Raffo, Karen Scott and Lucy Tiplady. Ivy led the work on cost benefit analysis, and Daniel led the analysis of NPD to which we refer in chapters five and six of this book. Any errors in reporting the cost benefit analysis and the NPD analysis are entirely ours. Much of the research we report here was guided by steering groups at the (then) DfES and DCSF. We would like to thank these groups for their advice. In particular, we are extremely grateful to the schools with whom we worked, and the members of staff, students, parents, local authority officers and members of other agencies who gave generously of their time.

Chapter 1

Full service and extended schools – an international movement?

Working beyond the school gates

In countries across the world, a new approach to schooling has begun to emerge in recent years which calls into question what we have historically believed schools to be and to be for. Like their counterparts elsewhere, schools adopting this approach focus primarily on teaching children, and therefore on helping children develop knowledge and skills in the classroom setting. However, these schools are not simply concerned with children as learners. They are also concerned with the personal, social and physical development of children, and with how they can access the services they need to support that development. They are concerned with how children thrive – or fail to thrive – within their families, and therefore with how families can best be engaged and supported. They are also concerned with the communities within which children and their families live, and how these communities in turn can offer the best support for children's development. In this sense, they define their role in terms not only of what happens in classrooms, but also of what happens beyond the school gates.

As a result, these schools tend to offer a range of services and activities which goes well beyond what other schools provide. In the USA, for instance, the Children's Aid Society describes what it calls 'community schools' as creating a 'web of support' for children based on three inter-connected systems:

A strong core instructional program designed to help all students meet high academic standards;

Enrichment activities designed to expand students' learning opportunities and to support their cognitive, social, emotional, moral and physical development;

A full range of health and mental health services designed to safeguard children's well-being and remove barriers to learning.

Some of the specific programs and services that may be found in community schools include extended-day instruction and enrichment, recreational and cultural programs, on-site health and mental health services, social services, parent support programs, adult education and teen programs. Typically, community schools are open during the regular school day as well as afternoons, evenings and weekends throughout the year, and the population they serve includes students, their families and the wider community. Parent involvement, participation and sanction are key to this process.

(Children's Aid Society, 2001, p. 16, emphasis in original)

The notion of a 'web of support' goes to the heart of what many of these schools seek to achieve, and what the circumstances are that have, in many cases, brought them into being. If, by 'support' we mean something like 'nurturant environments' (Irwin *et al.*, 2007, p. 3), then all children need support of some kind if they are to grow and learn. Such support comes primarily from their families, though peer groups, communities, child and family services, and, of course, schools also have a significant role to play. Community schools and others working in the same way, however, tend to assume that some children face such significant disadvantages that their hard-pressed families alone are unlikely to be able to create the kinds of highly nurturant environments they need. Child and family services, they argue, have to step into this breach. In particular, the schools themselves have to use their privileged position as key players in all children's lives to engage with families and communities, and to act as a hub for other services. Without doing so, indeed, they may not be able to effectively carry out their core task of promoting children's learning. As the prospectus for 'New (latterly, "Integrated") Community Schools' in Scotland puts it:

> Through New Community Schools we will make a radical attack on [the] vicious cycle of underachievement. New Community Schools will embody the fundamental principle that the potential of all children can be realised only by addressing their needs in the round – and that this requires an integrated approach by all those involved. Barriers to learning must be identified at the earliest stage, and intervention must be focused, planned and sustained. A range of services is necessary to assist children overcome the barriers to learning and positive development – family support, family learning and health improvement. New Community Schools will ensure that such expert advice and support is at hand – not at the end of a referral chain to other agencies.
>
> (The Scottish Office, 1998, foreword)

Not surprisingly, at a time when international comparisons have made countries acutely aware of equity issues in the educational achievements, well-being, and life chances of their children, initiatives such as these are appearing across a range of administrations. In recent years, for instance, there have been similar initiatives in many parts of the USA – particularly, though not exclusively, in the 'big cities' (see, for instance, Coalition for Community Schools, no date (b); Dryfoos and Quinn, 2005) – and in countries as diverse as Australia (Szirom *et al.*, 2001), Canada (see, for instance, M Tymchak [chair] Task Force and Public Dialogue on the Role of the School, 2001), the Irish Republic (Ryan, 2004), the Netherlands (The Dutch Community School Steering Group, 2004), South Africa (Department of Education. Directorate: Inclusive Education [Republic of South Africa], 2005), and, doubtless, many more. They all share the view that schools have to offer a wider range of services to children – and, typically, to their families and communities – than has traditionally been the case. For this reason, they are often referred to as 'full service' approaches to schooling (Dryfoos, 1994).

However, it is with the question of what such schools are to be called that the first hints of complexity enter the story. Although 'full service' school is a common label, recognizably similar approaches might also be called 'community' school, or 'multi-service' school, or 'school linked services', or 'SchoolPLUS', or 'Schools Plus', or 'extended' school. To complicate matters further, in some countries – Sweden is an obvious example (Cameron et al., 2009) – approaches of this kind have no special name because many schools offer additional services and activities as a matter of course; it is simply 'what schools do'. Even when the name is the same, the detail of what is on offer may be different. South African full service schools, for instance, do indeed offer a wide range of additional services like their counterparts in other countries – but primarily to children with difficulties and disabilities as an alternative to special school placement. Indeed, even within the same initiative and in the same administration, what individual schools offer may be quite different. As Joy Dryfoos, one of the pioneers of 'full service' schooling in the USA, puts it:

> Although the word 'model' is used a lot, in reality no two schools are alike; they are all different. The quality that is most compelling about community school philosophy is responsiveness to differences: in needs of populations to be served; in configurations of school staff; in capabilities of partner agencies; in capacity for change in community climate; and in availability of resources. These programs are always changing in response to changing conditions.
>
> (Dryfoos, 2005, p. vii)

Even our description of this approach to schooling as 'new' is somewhat problematic. It is certainly true that examples have multiplied in recent years, yet this is not an entirely new phenomenon. As early as the 1960s, when policy makers were looking to develop approaches of this kind amongst English primary schools, they were able to study established examples in Denmark, Poland, Russia, and the USA (Central Advisory Council for Education [England], 1967, par. 123). Certainly, in the USA, this approach has a long history, reaching back at least as far as the early part of the twentieth century, and having its roots in some quite fundamental assumptions about the role that schools should play in forging a democratic society (Dobbs, 2001; Richardson, 2009). As we shall shortly see, something similar could be said about the history of this approach in England – at least in terms of its length and the twists and turns it contains, even if the democratic imperative may not have been quite as marked.

Our concern here is to see what can be learned from these various attempts at broadening the role of schools. More specifically, we wish to examine critically the claims that changing what schools do in this way can have positive impacts on breaking the 'vicious cycle of underachievement', and can thereby contribute to greater social and educational equity. Such claims are, as we shall see, common in the policy and advocacy literature in this field. They are also exceedingly bold. It is well known that, even in affluent countries with well-resourced education systems, there is a stubborn link between childhood background, educational outcomes, and adult life chances (Raffo *et al.*, 2007; Wilkinson and Pickett, 2009). The strength of that link, and the inequalities into which children are born vary across countries, but schooling in its traditional form seems unable to level the playing field on which young people must begin their adult lives. If, therefore, changing the role of the school could break this link – or even weaken it significantly – that would be a remarkable achievement, and something of which all education systems would need to take note.

Evaluating such claims is no easy task when the approach to schooling out of which they arise does not even have an agreed name. For the purposes of this book, therefore, we have opted to combine the internationally recognized term 'full service schools' with the 'extended school' label that has been most widely used in England. The resulting hybrid – 'full service and extended schools' – may be somewhat inelegant and, as we shall see, is not without its conceptual problems, but it has the virtue of being likely to mean something to many of our readers. However, inventing a label of this kind cannot disguise the fact that it refers to many different initiatives, each taking a slightly different form, and each likely to be interpreted differently by participating schools. If there is indeed a full service and extended 'approach', it exists only at the level of some very broad principles – perhaps no more than a commitment to see learners in the classroom in the wider context of their lives outside those classrooms. Beyond this, the variability of this approach across time and place begs a series of questions. What additional services and activities should schools provide? How should they engage with families? What kind of working relationship should they have with other services – and, indeed, with which services? What kinds of education, social, and economic policies are needed to support schools working in this way? Above all, what evidence is there that the claims made for an approach of this kind are more than simply rhetorical?

We hope in this book to raise – and, so far as we are able, to answer – questions of this kind. Our conclusion is that full service and extended schools do indeed have much to contribute to efforts to tackle social and educational disadvantage. However, we also conclude that questions about the practicalities and impacts of such schools cannot adequately be answered without at the same time addressing some more fundamental issues. Widening the role of schools may do something to ameliorate the effects of disadvantage, but do we not also need to take into account everything we know about the structural causes of social and educational inequalities, and is it not improbable that schools alone can create more equal societies? Likewise, full service and extended schools may be able to support children, families and communities, but can we be entirely comfortable with the notion that school-based professionals know best what people living in disadvantaged circumstances need? Do we not have to take into account all we know about the power imbalances built into such an assumption, and about the tendency for professionals to view 'disadvantaged people' overwhelmingly in deficit terms? Above all, can we assess the role of schools in relation to social and educational disadvantage without also considering what kind of society we are trying to build, and what the role of schools might be in building this society?

Our positive conclusion about full service and extended school approaches is surrounded both by caveats and by possibilities. The caveats are about the limitations – and even dangers – of such approaches as we have known them hitherto. If, we conclude, such approaches have much to offer, what they can do is miniscule compared to the challenges posed by social and educational disadvantage, let alone by the task of creating more equal societies. Likewise, what they offer may be positively dangerous if it reinforces the relative powerlessness and marginalization of many people living in disadvantaged circumstances. On the other hand, the possibilities raised by full service and extended school approaches are also considerable. If, we argue, the work of schools can be aligned with more far-reaching efforts to tackle disadvantage, the potential for significant impacts is considerably increased. If, in particular, widening the role of the school can be taken as an opportunity to rethink what we expect from schools, there is the possibility of opening up a much-needed debate about how schools might help build our societies and, therefore, about what kind of societies we are trying to build.

Since the full service and extended schools 'movement' (if, indeed, it is such) is international in scope, we try wherever possible to consider these issues in the light of the international experience. However, precisely because such schools are outward-looking, their characteristics and approaches are shaped significantly by their local circumstances, and by the characteristics of the systems and services in relation to which they operate. For this reason, we wish to ground our arguments in a more detailed analysis of what has happened in our own country. England has a long history of schools seeking to work with children, families and communities outside their classrooms and beyond their gates – a history that illuminates many of the issues in this field. For a while in the 1980s and early 1990s, it seemed as though that history might have come to an end. However, during the years of the New Labour governments between 1997 and 2010, there was an upsurge in interest in 'extending' the role of schools, and we have been involved in a series of studies that have tracked and evaluated these developments. Our work in this field began over a decade ago, with a study of how schools did (or did not) contribute to the sustainability and regeneration of areas of concentrated social and educational disadvantage (Clark *et al.*, 1999; Crowther *et al.*, 2003). We were then able to trace a succession of government-sponsored pilot schemes (Cummings *et al.*, 2004; Dyson *et al.*, 2002), culminating in the 'Full Service Extended Schools' initiative (Cummings *et al.*, 2005, 2006, 2007a) from which much of the evidence we present in this book is drawn. Our work continues. At the time of writing, the developments begun under the New Labour governments continue under a different (Conservative–Liberal Democrat) administration, and we are evaluating a major policy initiative to ensure that all schools offer access to extended services (Cummings *et al.*, 2010).

Taken together, these initiatives have offered a unique opportunity to track developments over time across an entire national school system. Given that similar initiatives in most other parts of the world tend to be rather small-scale and localized, and, as we shall see, that evaluations in this field are typically small-scale and short-term, we believe that there is much to learn from this body of work. Moreover, it has become apparent that the initiatives in which we have been involved are part of a remarkable experiment, not only to turn every publicly funded school in the country into an extended school, but to incorporate the work of schools into a seamless network of child and family services. This attempt, for all its problematic aspects, has, we believe, opened up important new ways of thinking about the role of schools that we will return to towards the end of this book. It is, therefore, to the development of full service and extended schools in England that we now wish to turn.

The story in England

A remarkable experiment?

The full extent of the experiment taking place in England became clear when, in 2005, the Westminster government announced that every state-controlled school in the country would be expected to offer access for children and families to a 'core offer' of five 'extended services': childcare, out-of hours activities for students, parenting support, swifter referral to specialist services, and community access to school facilities (DfES, 2005b, p. 8). What makes this initiative remarkable is not so much the individual services and activities that schools are expected to offer. In fact, most schools in England have offered at least some of these in the past. Nor is it the combination of all of these services and activities in single schools. Again, there have long been examples of schools offering a range of services to children, families and communities. Rather, it is the scale and ambition of the experiment that is striking. The intention has been not simply to develop a few exceptional schools working beyond the standard remit, but to transform the entire school system into one able to meet the demands of education in the twenty-first century. As the government's manifesto for this new kind of school system put it:

> Schools rightly see their central purpose as preparing children and young people for life . . . However, now more than at any time in the past, a changing society and economy place great demands on our school system. The future will require more of today's young people to have higher-level skills and qualifications than ever before. It will require more of them to be equipped to cope with risk, uncertainty and change; and all of them to be able to make a positive contribution to an increasingly diverse society. We need young people to be prepared to face challenges and change; able to think, learn and work independently; able to show persistence and application; able to research in-depth; work with others, logically, analytically and creatively; and with the personal skills and attitudes to make a success of a range of personal circumstances. Meanwhile, as society becomes more diverse and complex and as family structures continue to change, schools now need to meet the needs of a much more diverse body of pupils, who bring to school a much wider range of backgrounds, experience, knowledge, beliefs

and assumptions than in the past . . . A world-leading education system fit for the 21st century must respond to these challenges.

(DCSF, 2008a, pp. 11–12)

In this respect, as in so many others over the past two decades, the English education system is acting as what some US researchers have described as a kind of educational 'laboratory', where the effects of bold and ambitious reforms can be observed by other countries (Finkelstein and Grubb, 2000). Many working in the English system would doubtless argue that these reforms are often more problematic than at first they seem, and are rarely as successful as their proponents tend to claim. Nonetheless, their interest and significance for policy makers and practitioners elsewhere is beyond doubt.

The historical context

Despite the policy rhetoric about '21st century schools' (DCSF, 2008a), the idea that schools should do more than simply teach children in classrooms, and that they should have some kind of wider involvement with children's lives, with their parents, and with the communities in which they live, in fact has a venerable history in the English school system. Just where this history starts is a matter for debate. Schools in England have long been seen as in some important way part of the communities they serve, and local people have been expected to have a voice in running them ever since the introduction of universal elementary education in 1870 (Sallis, 2000, p. 4). Throughout this period, schools have, to a greater or lesser extent, offered clubs and cultural and sporting activities to their students, invited parents in to discuss their children's progress, raise funds for the school, and attend school performances, and acted as bridges between children, families and the doctors, nurses, social workers and other professionals who could provide them with non-educational services. In a sense, therefore, what have come in recent years to be called full service or extended schools are simply examples of long-established practices being taken to their logical conclusion.

The first large-scale attempt to make this kind of extended provision central to the work of schools is generally accepted as having taken place in the period between the First and Second World Wars and to have been led by the then chief education officer of Cambridgeshire, Henry Morris (Jeffs, 1999). Cambridgeshire is now known as a rather affluent and attractive part of the country, within easy commuting distance of London, its prosperity built on the knowledge industries centred on the historic University of Cambridge. In the 1920s, however, the situation was very different, as rural poverty was rife and former agricultural workers migrated to towns and cities to find better employment. Morris took the view that the education service could and should not detach itself from the fate of the county as a whole. He accordingly proposed the establishment of a series of 'Village Colleges' which would act both as schools in the traditional sense, and as hubs for the educational, cultural and social life of the community. By building a range of social resources into the fabric of the major public institution in the village, Morris reasoned, it ought to be possible to enhance the quality of rural life, equip the rural worker with new skills, and put an end to the drift of population towards urban settings. As his famous Memorandum put it, the Village College:

> would take all the various vital but isolated activities in village life – the School, the Village Hall and Reading Room, the Evening Classes, the Agricultural Education Courses, the Women's Institute, the British Legion, Boy Scouts and Girl Guides, the recreation ground, the branch of the County Rural Library, the Athletic and Recreation Clubs – and, bringing them together into relation, create a new institution for the English countryside. It would create out of discrete elements an organic whole; the vitality of the constituent elements would be preserved, and not destroyed, but the unity they would form would be a new thing. For, as in the case of all organic unities, the whole is greater than the mere sum of the parts. It would be a true social synthesis – it would take existing and live elements and bring them into a new and unique relationship.
>
> (Morris, 1924, p. XV)

Although it is customary to see Morris as an educational visionary, his plans were in fact eminently practical. Despite considerable difficulties, five colleges had opened by the time he retired in 1954, with a further seven opening under his successor (Turner, 1972). Moreover, Village Colleges continue to form an important part of the Cambridgeshire school system. Whilst the communities they serve and the understandings of what it means to serve those communities have undoubtedly changed, they still act as community hubs, bringing together a range of services and activities for children, families and residents. Indeed, some of them have served as pilot schools for the more recent development of extended schools (Dyson et al., 2002).

Not surprisingly, therefore, the Cambridgeshire model, in different guises, was subsequently taken up in a range of other local education authorities such as Devon, Coventry, Leicestershire and Northumberland. In many places, the model was adopted in a relatively conservative form. Schools hosted adult learning and leisure activities on site, but otherwise there was no real change to the way they worked. Elsewhere, however, the traditional model of schooling came under a much more rigorous and critical examination. In the 1970s particularly, as the selective system of secondary education was replaced by 'comprehensive' schools catering for all children living in their areas (Benn and Simon, 1972), many elements of traditional schooling were coming into question. Across the country schools and colleges – Countesthorpe College in Leicestershire (Watts, 1974) being probably the most famous (or notorious, depending on one's point of view) – took the breaking of the boundary between school and community as a starting point for testing other boundaries in and around the school. New relationships with families and communities, therefore, combined with new forms of organization, new models of curriculum, more democratic forms of governance and more open teacher–student relations in a more or less radical attempt to rethink the school (Moon, 1983).

Although some of the most adventurous attempts at boundary-testing took place in the secondary sector, there was also considerable thought devoted to the future of primary education. The Plowden Report on primary schooling (Central Advisory Council for Education [England], 1967), placed the emphasis on what came to be known (sometimes pejoratively) as 'child-centred' approaches. It recommended that schools should pay greater attention to children as individuals very different from one another, and developing organically not just in the classroom, but also in family and community environments. For many children, these environments were sufficiently nurturing children to grow and learn appropriately. For some, however, the social and economic disadvantages they faced meant that schools needed to intervene to offer additional support. Two sets of recommendations that are of interest to us emerged from this view. First, Plowden argued that the level of medical and social care services for children should be increased, that schools should develop closer partnerships with professionals in these services, and that some of these professionals might, under certain circumstances, be based in schools (Central Advisory Council for Education [England], 1967, cp. 7). Although Plowden did not quite go so far as to advocate the establishment of 'full service' schools in the modern sense, it seemed clear that schools offered a point through which non-educational services could access children and their families. As a subsequent review child health services (DHSS, 1976) put it:'The length of time that the majority of children spend at school makes it a unique setting in which preventative and remedial work may be carried out' (Committee on Child Health Services [SDM Court chair], 1976, section 10.58). Second, Plowden argued that all schools should pay greater attention to parental involvement and to the facilities and opportunities available in the communities where their students live. In particular, the Report argued for the development of 'community schools'. 'School buildings and grounds represent an immense capital investment which has been provided by the community', reasoned Plowden, and therefore,

> the community should have such access to them as is compatible with their effective daytime use. . . . We therefore hope that attempts of many different kinds will be made to use primary schools out of ordinary hours . . . Children can be given opportunities during a late afternoon session and in the daytime during holidays for carrying on their hobbies and for expression in the arts and for games. Parents can be invited to the school in the evenings to learn about its ways and to make things that will be useful for the school. Parents and others in the community should help to organise activities and staff the school during its late afternoon session, just as they have rallied to provide play groups and to support youth clubs.
> (Central Advisory Council for Education [England], 1967, pars. 124–26)

The matters of service delivery, parental partnership and community facilities were, Plowden judged, particularly pressing in the most disadvantaged parts of towns and cities. The report therefore advocated for the designation of such places as

'Educational Priority Areas' (EPAs) where additional resources could be directed, the community school idea could be piloted, and schools could be encouraged to experiment with new approaches to tackling the effects of disadvantage.

In many ways, therefore, the elements of a distinctive model of full service and extended schooling were in place in England by the late 1970s. The radical approach of some community colleges was paralleled by equally radical experimentation with community-oriented education in EPAs (see, for instance, Midwinter, 1973). At the same time, there was the potential, at least, for combining these educational experiments with more collaborative working between schools and other services. However, developments of this kind were short-lived. Educational Priority Areas lasted only a few years, with little evidence that they had transformed either schools or the disadvantaged communities they served (Smith, 1987). Almost before they were born, doubts began to be raised about whether education could in fact 'compensate for society' (Bernstein, 1970), or whether it ought not instead to concentrate on its core business of teaching children as effectively as possible. So-called 'progressive' education came under increasing attack from those who worried that it threatened traditional standards of attainment and behaviour (see, for instance, Cox and Dyson, 1971), and even the Prime Minister could be heard worrying aloud about whether the 'balance' of the school system had gone awry (Callaghan, 1976). Not surprisingly, perhaps, the enthusiasm for boundary-testing schools began to wane, and attention came to be focused increasingly on the internal processes of the school, and their effectiveness in driving up attainments in the 'core' curriculum. The election of a Conservative government under Margaret Thatcher in 1979 effectively signalled the end of any government support for community schooling. The subsequent introduction of a major reform of the school system, in the form of the 1988 Education Reform Act, brought about a radical reorientation of the aims of schooling and the relationship between schools, families and communities.

The story of the 1988 Act has been told often enough for it not to detain us too long here (see Bash and Coulby, 1989 for an early account, and Ball, 2008 for a more recent reappraisal). From our point of view, the key provisions were: that it laid out a prescribed national curriculum, and so ended any thought of experimentation with basing what was taught on 'community' relevance or interest; that it gave schools considerably more autonomy *vis à vis* the local authorities who had overall responsibility for the well-being of their areas; and that it cast parents as 'consumers' of education, choosing, if they wished, to send their children to schools some distance away from where the family lived. Taken together, these measures served to reshape, and in many ways to weaken, the links between schools and the communities they served. On the one hand, schools became answerable to national imperatives – a prescriptive curriculum, the performance of their students in national tests, the attentions of a national schools inspectorate (Ofsted) – rather than to the direction of their democratically controlled local authority. On the other hand, the school ceased to be the place where all the local community's children were educated, and instead became a quasi-business, recruiting students wherever it could find them. Not surprisingly, by the time these reforms had fully worked their way through the system, relatively few schools were recruiting students from single, cohesive areas (Chamberlain *et al.*, 2006).

It is important, however, not to overstate these impacts. The pre-1988 system was no idyll in which schools related unproblematically to clearly defined communities and paid close attention to the wishes of parents and community members. Moreover, although national policies undoubtedly impacted on schools' work, many of the initiatives that had developed during the 1960s and 1970s survived in some form or other and, in some cases, flourished. When a 'New' Labour government was elected in 1997, therefore, it found a situation in which many schools were continuing to explore the additional activities and services they could offer, though they tended to be doing so in an opportunistic manner, without real national – or indeed local – coordination (Ball, 1998; Wilkin *et al.*, 2003a).

New Labour and extended schools

Again, the broad thrust of New Labour education policy is well enough known not to detail us here (for a recent survey, see Chapman and Gunter, 2009). Prior to taking office as Prime Minister, Tony Blair famously declared his three priorities to be 'education, education, and education' (Blair, 1996), and once in office, he set about launching, an 'unprecedented crusade to raise standards' (Blair, 1999). The principal features of previous Conservative policy – the marketized system of families 'choosing' schools, the 'freeing' of schools from local authority control, the regular assessment of children's attainments, the trust in central direction and mistrust of local authorities, and the use of high stakes accountability as an instrument of school improvement – were all retained and, in many cases, intensified as the basis of this crusade (Phillips and Harper-Jones, 2003). What is sometimes overlooked, though, is that these continued efforts at system reform were accompanied by policies directed at overcoming educational disadvantage, and that these were themselves part of a broader policy imperative to tackle social disadvantage.

New Labour's commitment to education was based on the belief that, in the context of economic globalization, a high-wage economy such as that of the UK could only hope to be competitive if its workers were able to sell high levels of skill and knowledge rather than simply relying on selling their labour cheaply. As Blair put it:

> . . . we cannot hope to prosper as a nation if we do not educate all our citizens properly.
>
> (Blair, 2005)

However, the phrase 'all our citizens' was not accidental. New Labour were convinced that the nation could not be prosperous whilst significant numbers of people remained low-skilled and, by the same token, that the surest way for individual citizens to enhance their own prospects was for them to develop their knowledge and skills. 'That is why', as one Secretary of State for Education and Skills, Ruth Kelly, explained,

> I see my department as the department for life chances. And that is why I see it
> as my job to boost social mobility . . . Our task is to make sure that for everyone
> involved in learning, excellence and equity become and remain reality.
>
> (Kelly, 2005)

With this in mind, New Labour governments set about finding ways of ensuring educational 'excellence for the many, not just the few' (Blunkett, 1999). To some extent, this was to be achieved by improvements in the education system overall, on the assumption that better schools and better teaching must necessarily benefit those who historically had done least well. However, New Labour were particularly concerned by groups who were – or were at risk of becoming – 'socially excluded'. They characterized this condition as:

> . . . what can happen when people or areas have a combination of problems, such
> as unemployment, discrimination, poor skills, low incomes, poor housing, high
> crime and family breakdown. These problems are linked and mutually reinforc-
> ing. Social exclusion is an extreme consequence of what happens when people
> do not get a fair deal throughout their lives and find themselves in difficult situ-
> ations. This pattern of disadvantage can be transmitted from one generation to
> the next.
>
> (Social Exclusion Task Force, 2009)

For those at risk of social exclusion, education offered the surest means of cutting through the knot of problems which they faced (Blunkett, 1999). However, those problems were so acute that system-wide improvement alone would not be enough. Government, therefore, set about devising and deploying a rapid succession of interventions targeted at particular groups of learners, or at the schools where such learners were concentrated (Antoniou *et al.*, 2008).

As the aforementioned definition implies, the idea of social exclusion carried an assumption that there are certain areas – notably, the poorer parts of towns and cities – where the intersection of multiple disadvantages are most likely to occur. What was needed, therefore, was a multi-strand package of interventions aimed at dealing with each of the complex problems of such areas. Accordingly, one of the major tasks of the first New Labour government was to set about developing a 'National Strategy for Neighbourhood Renewal' by commissioning a series of 'Policy Action Teams' to investigate different aspects of social exclusion in these areas and recommend the kind of interventions that might have been tried (Social Exclusion Unit, 1998, 2000, 2001). Given the interacting nature of problems in these areas, the expectation was that the interventions formulated by the different team would be mutually reinforcing, and therefore that it would be important to ensure that they were properly 'joined up'. Indeed, one team was commissioned to look specifically at how this might be achieved (National Strategy for Neighbourhood Renewal, 2000).

Since education was seen as the principal pathway out of exclusion, it is not surprising that one of the action teams was concerned with the role of schools in disadvantaged areas. However, in the spirit of 'joining up', the 'Schools Plus' team was concerned not just with how the internal practices of schools might be improved, but also with what schools might do that would contribute to the regeneration of the areas they served (DfEE, 1999). What emerged was:

> a vision of these schools in the future as centres of excellence for community involvement with more services on site or co-located. Other agencies and bodies would provide integrated support for pupils and offer complementary learning activities. Budgets would be focused at school level, and schools would be resourced to offer flexible individual learning programmes and to have close links to other phases of education. Clear achievement and other targets would be set and monitored.
>
> (DfEE, 1999, p. 6)

In a pattern that would become familiar as the extended schools agenda developed in England, the team identified a diverse set of activities and services that schools were to be encouraged to adopt, and that would, it hoped, realize this vision in some coherent way. So, it argued, schools in disadvantaged areas should offer study support and adult learning opportunities, provide a base for other child, family and community services, promote parental involvement, instigate links with local businesses, and develop the involvement of young people in their local communities. Whilst some of these activities were new and reflected developments over the 1980s and 1990s, the proposals were, to all intents and purposes, a reworking of the community school developments of earlier decades.

The Schools Plus report marked the beginning of a sustained attempt to explore what community schooling might mean in the educational context of the new millennium. Over the next few years, various pilot projects were commissioned to encourage schools to develop a wider role, or to learn from schools – such as the Village Colleges – where such a role had been established many years ago (Cummings *et al.*, 2004; Dyson *et al.*, 2002; Shaw *et al.*, 2003). The most significant of these was the Full Service Extended Schools (FSES) project, which ran between 2003 and 2006, and which we were asked to evaluate (Cummings *et al.*, 2005, 2006, 2007a). In its original form, the FSES initiative envisaged that one school would be identified in each local authority area for development as a full service school. By the time the project had run its course, nearly 150 schools had participated, the majority of them serving highly disadvantaged areas. Each school received relatively generous additional funding (up to £162,000 in the first year), but was expected to supplement this with funding and resources secured from other sources, and to ensure that its provision was self-sustaining by the end of the project. In return for funding, the schools were expected to develop a diverse range of services and activities much like that recommended in the Schools Plus report: the provision of childcare facilities, collaboration with health and social care services, adult and family learning opportunities, parenting support, study support, and access for children and adults to sport, arts, and information and communications technology (ICT) facilities and activities. It was a matter for individual schools to decide the detail of what these services should look like in their own circumstances. However, it was assumed that, in order to make them available, schools would need to stay open beyond the school day and school year, and that their facilities would be accessible to families and community members as well as to their students.

Before the FSES project had finished, the government announced a major extension and reorientation of its plans to develop 'extended services' in and around schools (DfES, 2005b). For the first time, the expectation was that all schools, rather than just a few volunteer institutions, would offer additional services and activities. Once again, a 'core offer' of services was specified: out of hours activities for children, childcare provision, parenting support and family learning, community access to facilities and adult learning opportunities, and 'swift and easy' access for children to specialist services. Again, schools were free to decide precisely how they would configure these services, and there was an expectation that they would stay open beyond the normal school day and year. On the other hand, in a break with previous initiatives, there was no expectation that every school would offer every service on its own site. Instead, schools were encouraged to work together in clusters, to collaborate with other service providers in their area, and to direct ('signpost' in the jargon) children and families to services across the area. Although most schools would doubtless wish to provide one or more services themselves, the test was not what the school provided, but what potential service users could access.

Even with this caveat, the extended services agenda as it emerged in 2005 and as it is now being rolled out across the country is, as we indicated earlier, a remarkable experiment. It is one thing to encourage individual schools to develop extended provision as a response to evident problems in their student populations and in the communities they serve. It is quite another to expect all schools to become involved, including those serving more affluent areas where local people face none of the intersecting problems of social exclusion. In order to understand what seems like a sudden shift in focus, therefore, it is necessary to locate the new extended services agenda in relation to a wider policy context.

New Labour was fond – some would say, excessively fond – of interventions targeted at disadvantaged places and people. However, it also consistently espoused the principle of 'progressive universalism', defined succinctly by former Deputy Prime Minister, John Prescott, as 'universal because we aim to help everyone; . . . and progressive because we aim to do more for those who need it most' (Prescott, 2002). In effect, progressive universalism means devising public services, welfare systems and fiscal regimes which support the whole population, but which are sufficiently flexible to direct most resources and support at those in greatest need. A prime example would be the National Health Service in England, which is more or less freely available to all, but which is capable of targeting most resources at those who are most seriously ill, or most at risk of ill-health. Progressive universalism in this sense replaces the sharp dividing lines between those who do and do not receive a service with a continuum of service provision. In principle, at least, this is a flexible and efficient way to deliver services which avoids 'all or nothing' decisions about who gets what. With this in mind, it makes sense for extended services to be available in and around all schools rather than to create oases of provision in some places and deserts in others.

However, this development is only possible in the context of another example of New Labour's progressive universalist approach – the Every Child Matters (ECM) initiative (DfES, 2003a). ECM constitutes nothing less than a fundamental reform of health, social care, education and other services for children to make them as integrated and coherent as possible. As such, it revisits the themes of service integration that surfaced some three decades earlier in the Plowden (Central Advisory Council for Education [England], 1967) and Court (Committee on Child Health Services [SDM Court chair], 1976) reports. The rationale for the reform programme is that services for children and their families have traditionally been managed in 'silos', and divided between separate organizations and institutions in a way that is both inefficient and ineffective:

> Our existing system for supporting children and young people who are beginning to experience difficulties is often poorly co-ordinated and accountability is unclear. This means that information is not shared between agencies so that warning signs are not recognised and acted upon. Some children are assessed many times by different agencies and despite this may get no services. Children may experience a range of professionals involved in their lives but little continuity and consistency of support. Organisations may disagree over who should pay for meeting a child's needs because their problems cut across organisational boundaries. Fragmentation locally is often driven by conflicting messages and competing priorities from central Government.
>
> (DfES, 2003a, pp. 21–22)

On this basis, governments have, in recent years, required local authorities to bring their child and family services together into integrated children's services departments, created mechanisms (so-called 'children's trusts') for coordinating these and other services at local level, formulated a set of shared 'outcomes' which all services are expected to promote, and tried to develop shared practices across services, particularly in respect of assessment.

The basis of these newly integrated services is 'universalist' in that all children are expected to access them to some degree, but 'progressive' in that more intensive and specialist services can be directed at those children facing greatest levels of difficulty. In this context, the role of schools is crucial. As a universal service, schools offer both a means of providing a minimum level of service to all children, and a point through which children can access and be accessed by whatever additional services they need. As government guidance explains:

Extended schools are a key vehicle for delivering the Government's objective of lifting children out of poverty and improving outcomes for them and their families . . . A key priority, and challenge, for schools is to reach the most disadvantaged families within a universal framework of providing mainstream services for all families.

(HM Government, 2007, p. 2)

In practice, this means that schools are being asked to take on increasingly wide-ranging roles in relation to all of their students. So, for instance, they may be asked to work on children's health (DCSF, 2008c) and on their emotional well-being (Humphrey *et al.*, 2008) as well as on their academic attainments. It also means that they are expected to act as hubs for referrals to other services. Increasingly, therefore, local authorities are organizing their children's services in area-based teams, more or less closely linked to schools in each area, and schools are creating their own multi-professional teams to meet what they see as the needs of their students (Cummings *et al.*, 2007b).

The same principles apply to the role of schools in relation to families and communities. There is, for instance, a national childcare strategy which is also built on progressive universalist assumptions (DfEE and DSS, 1998). Whilst all families are likely to need childcare of some kind, the need for publicly provided care becomes more acute where children have impoverished experiences in the home or where parents – particularly women – need access to childcare so that they can work and break out of poverty. In this context, schools offer an attractive, locally based setting where they can either provide childcare themselves or ensure that parents know how to access the service they need (DfES, 2002a). In the same way, all communities need to be cohesive, and some, where there are significant tensions and conflicts, call for positive interventions. Schools, therefore, have been given a duty to promote 'community cohesion' (DCSF, 2007) on the assumption that all will need to do something to prepare their students for living in a diverse society, but some will need to be involved in vigorous interventions to address issues in their areas.

The logical implication of this is that the wider role for schools developed here and there by previous initiatives needs to become part of the way that all schools operate. It may remain the case that only a minority will become 'full service' schools in the sense that they offer a wide range of child, family and community services on the school site. However, all will become part of a 'full service system' in the sense that they will be seamlessly integrated with, and will contribute to, a readily accessible network of such services.

Raising the issues

When we look at the recent upsurge of activity around extended schools and services, and the parallel activities in many other countries, it is, on one level, difficult to disagree with the claim by the Full-service Schools Roundtable in Boston, USA, that 'Full-service schools is an idea whose time has come' (Full-service Schools Roundtable).

It certainly seems to be the case that in a range of countries, educators and policy makers have come to the conclusion that it is not enough for schools simply to focus on delivering an academic curriculum to their students in ordinary classrooms and in the course of a standard school day. If children are to do well, they need access to far more activities and services than this traditional model is able to offer, and schools offer an excellent base from which those services can be made available to them, to their families, and to the communities within which they live.

Yet the brief account we have given of the history of full service and extended approaches in England suggests that the story may be more complex than this. It is, for instance, clear that such approaches do indeed have a history, and that efforts to broaden the role of schools have been taking place in England, as in the USA, for the best part of a century. It is also clear that the nature of such efforts changes over time. Far from being 'an idea whose time has come', full service and extended schools are informed by ideas which change over time. Moreover, the history of such approaches emerges from the constantly changing context of the politics of education. Whether these approaches are in or out of fashion, and what form of those approaches seems most attractive depends, it would appear, on who has power and leadership in the education system, on the social circumstances they encounter, and on the dominant social and educational values to which they adhere. Henry Morris's crusade to save the community life of rural Cambridgeshire is very different in these respects from the New Labour government's efforts to supplement their 'crusade to raise standards'. Both, of course, are different again from the post-1979 Conservative government's focus on internal school system reform which left little space for engaging schools in family and community issues. As if to underline this point, New Labour has recently lost power in England, and it seems almost inevitable that the new government will, in due course, rethink once again the relationship between schools, families and communities.

If, moreover, full service and extended approaches cannot be divorced from the social and political contexts in which they arise, neither can they be divorced from the way fundamental questions about the purposes of education are answered. We argued earlier that such approaches raised issues in relation to the origins of disadvantage, the role of schools, and the nature of the society to which schools are expected to contribute. We can now see a little more clearly the kinds of questions we might need to ask in order to explore these issues. From Henry Morris, for instance, we can add questions about the kind of community life schools should support. From Plowden we can add questions about how children grow and develop, what the role of the family might be in this process, and how schools should work with families. From New Labour we can add questions about whether policy should target disadvantaged groups and places, or should embody 'progressive universalism', or should embody some other principle of equity.

The organization of the book

Throughout this book we will find ourselves brought back to questions of this kind. Whilst much of what we have to say concerns the practices and outcomes of extended school initiatives in England, we will also need to address issues of disadvantage and equity, professionalism and power, schools of the future and, above all, the nature of the 'good society'. In other words, we will need to get beneath the surface appearance of full service and extended schools in order to uncover the responses they embody to these issues. We begin this process in the next chapter by looking more closely at the rationales that policy makers and advocates have offered for extending the role of schools, and at the assumptions on which such rationales are based.

In chapter three, we turn to a more detailed account of the Full Service Extended Schools initiative in England, and present accounts of how schools within this initiative organized themselves and what they tried to achieve. The FSES initiative remains our focus for the three subsequent chapters. In chapter four, we consider the challenges that FSESs faced in realizing their approaches and the implications of these challenges for full service and extended schools elsewhere. In chapter five, we turn to the vexed issue of how the impacts of such schools can be assessed. We describe how we set about evaluating FSESs and consider how our approach might be used both by other evaluators and by leaders of full service and extended schools themselves. In chapter six we discuss what we found to be the outcomes of FSESs and set our findings in the context of the international evaluation evidence. Finally, in chapter seven we broaden our focus from the FSES initiative in England to the international experience with full service and extended schools. We consider the limitations of those schools as we have known them hitherto, but also set out what we see as some promising signs of how the determination to work 'beyond the school gates' might be developed in future. Throughout the book there are case studies and references to particular schools and other institutions, and quotes from individuals. These have been anonymized, and in all cases where names are used these are pseudonyms.

Our arguments throughout are addressed primarily to those who are trying to make a difference to the lives of children, families and communities. These may be practitioners and policy makers, but they may also be local leaders, community activists, or community members themselves. However, in this complex field, we see no distinction between what are sometimes taken to be the practical concerns of such groups and the more theoretical and critical concerns that often characterize the work of researchers. So far as we are concerned, wanting to make a difference necessarily involves asking what difference needs to be made – and vice versa. This book is, therefore, neither a 'how to do it' manual for school leaders, nor a research tract addressed only to academics. Rather, it seeks to bring the two sets of concerns together, in the conviction that things could be different, but only if action and research learn how to inform one another.

Chapter 2

What are they for?

Much of the energy that has surrounded international developments in the field of full service and extended schools in recent years has been focused on the practicalities of organizing activities and services. Much less attention has been paid to exploring what such schools are for or what they might realistically hope to achieve. As we saw in the previous chapter, initiatives in England particularly tend to have been specified in terms of a list of components which participating schools are expected to put in place. This, for instance, is the specification for the current extended services initiative:

- high quality 'wraparound' childcare provided on the school site or through other local providers, with supervised transfer arrangements where appropriate, available 8am–6pm all year round
- a varied menu of activities to be on offer such as homework clubs and study support, sport (at least two hours a week beyond the school day for those who want it), music tuition, dance and drama, arts and crafts, special interest clubs such as chess and first aid courses, visits to museums and galleries, learning a foreign language, volunteering, business and enterprise activities
- parenting support including information sessions for parents at key transition points, parenting programmes run with the support of other children's services and family learning sessions to allow children to learn with their parents
- swift and easy referral to a wide range of specialist support services such as speech therapy, child and adolescent mental health services, family support services, intensive behaviour support, and (for young people) sexual health services. Some may be delivered on school sites
- providing wider community access to ICT, sports and arts facilities, including adult learning

(DfES, 2005b, p. 8)

At one level, this is surprisingly detailed – major components are specified, activities are listed, hours are prescribed. However, it raises more questions than it answers. Out of the list of possible services and activities, which ones should a particular school offer, what emphasis should it place on each, and how, if at all, should they be linked to each other? On these points, the guidance declines to be specific, suggesting instead that:

> Schools will want to work closely with parents to shape these activities around the needs of their community and may choose to provide extra services in response to parental demand [. . .] there is no blueprint for the types of activities that schools might offer. How these services look and are delivered in or through a particular school will vary.
>
> (DfES, 2005b, p. 8)

Again, this raises more questions than it answers. What needs, precisely, should schools be responding to? How should they set about determining these needs? How should they balance 'needs' and 'parental demand' (and, indeed, why is parental demand important, whilst student demand, seemingly, is not)?

In these circumstances, it is not surprising that the leaders of each school tend to build services and activities on the basis of a diverse set of assumptions about what matters and why. When, for instance, we asked leaders of schools in the Full Service Extended Schools initiative why they were developing particular configurations of provision, they cited a wide range of aims and purposes – offering students greater opportunities for learning, making external services more readily available, enabling early interventions in students' problems, responding to a changing school population, enhancing community support for the school, building community cohesion, developing students' self-esteem, and many more (Cummings *et al.*, 2005, p. 11). This somewhat diverse set of aims perhaps reflects the fact that, even when government guidance addresses the question of what such schools are for, all that is on offer is a diverse list of anticipated – but unsubstantiated – outcomes. So, we are told that providing access to extended services through schools:

- supports improvement in standards
- enables children to have fun and develop wider interests/new skills
- enhances support for vulnerable children and those most at risk
- encourages greater parental involvement in children's learning
- makes better use of our school facilities by opening up sports, arts and ICT facilities to the community
- provides better help to staff and parents to address children's wider needs, such as support from visiting multi-agency teams
- provides additional opportunities for staff in schools for example, child-care and support staff may be interested in additional work in some of the services
- enables parents to return to work and so reduces the number of children living in poverty
- reduces health inequality through greater take up of school-based health and social care services such as smoking cessation clubs or midwifery services

(DfES, 2005b, p. 16)

Why these impacts are important, which are priorities, how they relate to other imperatives in education policy – these and many other questions are simply left unanswered.

It is, perhaps, a little unfair to single out initiatives in England, when in fact many attempts to develop full service approaches rest on a similar mixture of tight prescription of detail and loose specification of aims. The Eisenhower Foundation in the USA, for instance, offers the following guidance on its 'model' of full service community schools:

> Full-service community schools are characterized by: (1) Abundant individual attention, (2) Respect and high expectations for students, (3) High degree of parental involvement and services for parents, (4) Presence of health centers and family resource rooms, (5) After-school activities, (6) Cultural and community activities, (7) Extended hours – open from early in the morning until night, weekends and summers . . . While there is no one way to build full-service community schools, these schools share key principles: (1) Fostering strong partnerships, (2) Sharing accountability for results, (3) Setting high expectations for all, (4) Building on the community strengths, (5) Embracing diversity . . . Full-service community schools free teachers to teach by integrating critical child and family services into the fundamental design of the school. Full-service community schools respond to the changing roles of families and schools by providing vital support to both and strengthening the relationship between them.
>
> (Eisenhower Foundation, 2005, p. 6)

In the same vein, the Coalition for Community Schools offers a mixture of tight and loose specification of components, together with tantalizing promises of rather generalized outcomes:

> A wide range of models and approaches can fit into a basic community school framework. Every school is unique, but here's the Coalition's broad vision of a well-developed community school.
>
> A community school, operating in a public school building, is open to students, families and the community before, during and after school, seven days a week, all year long. It is operated jointly through a partnership between the school system and one or more community agencies. Families, youth, principals, teachers and neighborhood residents help design and implement activities that promote high educational achievement and use the community as a resource for learning.
>
> The school is oriented toward the community, encouraging student learning through community service and service learning. A before- and after-school learning component allows students to build on their classroom experiences, expand their horizons, contribute to their communities and have fun. A family support center helps families with child-rearing, employment, housing and other services. Medical, dental and mental health services are readily accessible.

Artists, lawyers, psychologists, college faculty and students, businesspeople, neighbors, and family members come to support and bolster what schools are working hard to accomplish – ensuring young people's academic, interpersonal and career success. Their presence turns schools into places that crackle with the excitement of doing, experiencing and discovering unknown talents and strengths. Community schools open up new channels for learning and self expression. Students come early and stay late – because they want to.

(Coalition for Community Schools, no date (a))

Superficially, such articulations of what community schools are and the purposes they serve are convincing. As with government guidance in England, however, scratching the surface of these texts raises more questions than it answers. What, for instance are the 'changing roles of families and schools', what kind of 'support' do they each need, and what, precisely, should be the nature of the 'relationship between them'? What are the 'new channels for learning and self expression' that community schools should open up? Why, precisely, are 'community service and service learning' so important? What is the source of the 'academic, interpersonal and career success' of students, and how, precisely are external visitors expected to contribute to this?

Whilst it is possible to hazard a guess at how these questions might be answered, those who draft guidance documents of this kind appear to assume that they do not need to make their own answers explicit. A recent review of initiatives in the UK aimed at tackling social and educational disadvantage claims that this lack of clarity is in fact, very typical (Griggs *et al.*, 2008). Such initiatives, it claims, are often based on post-hoc rationalization rather than a clear articulation of what they are intended to achieve. The authors of the review quote approvingly, therefore, an account of how such an articulation should be constructed:

Good strategy and project development means developing a 'theory of change'. This means being clear why you think things have happened in the way they have and developing a 'theory' of why your planned intervention might change things. There needs to be a logic to the change which joins up your definition of the problem with a logical reason why a particular course of action might help solve the problem. This 'theory of change' should inform your development of the project and allow you – in evaluation – to test whether your theory was right.

(Renewal Trust, no date, cited in Griggs *et al.*, 2008, p. 57)

In a situation where guidance documents leave so many questions unanswered, this notion of 'theory of change' is a useful way to explore the rationales on which full service and extended school initiatives are based. Our own studies have made extensive use of theory of change methodology as an approach to evaluation, and we will have much more to say about this when we discuss evaluation matters in chapter 5. Suffice it to say for now that our experience is that school leaders rarely have a fully explicit theory of this kind with which to guide the development of their schools. However, they do have more or less implicit sets of assumptions about what the problems are they are trying to solve, and how developing a full service or extended approach will help solve that problem. Much of our work, therefore, has been about working with them to surface these implicit theories of change.

It is possible to view larger-scale initiatives in much the same light. However problematic the guidance offered by leaders of such initiatives might be, what they are advising or requiring schools to do *implies* a theory of change. As they begin to speak about what children need to develop properly, or the problems of social exclusion, or what constitutes a thriving community, we can begin to discern the outlines of those theories. By surfacing the theories that they imply, we can begin to answer some of the questions on which initiative leaders themselves may remain silent. We can, more importantly, ultimately link the surface features of full service and extended school approaches to underpinning views about the nature of the social world, the role of education, and the kind of society that schools should help to build – and in this way begin to consider the issues we started to raise in the previous chapter. As we do so, we shall find that, not only are such approaches configured differently, but that they rest on fundamentally different perspectives on these matters. It is to this task that we now turn.

Surfacing theories of change

That such divergences exist is already apparent in the Plowden report's (Central Advisory Council for Education [England], 1967) advocacy of community schools, which we outlined in chapter one. For the most part, Plowden had a rather positive view of the relationship between children, parents and schools. Put simply, most parents already support their children's development and learning, and will do so even more if they see their child learning successfully. All schools have to do, therefore, is to encourage the naturally supportive tendencies of parents by enabling their children to learn as successfully as possible. 'Schools', the report asserts, 'exist to foster virtuous circles' (ibid. para 103). If there is a problem in this situation, it is simply that parents demand too little from their schools (ibid. para 106).

However, the tone changes abruptly when Plowden discusses those areas of social and educational disadvantage where community schools are to be developed as a priority. Here, poverty, poor housing, inadequate schools, and difficulties in teacher recruitment produce dire conditions. There are no 'virtuous circles'. Rather:

> Teachers must be constantly aware that ideas, values and relationships within the school may conflict with those of the home, and that the world assumed by teachers and school books may be unreal to the children. There will have to be constant communication between parents and the school if the aims of the school are to be fully understood.
>
> (ibid. para 136)

Community schools in these areas, it would appear, will need to overcome the dysfunctional culture of home and community, as well as offsetting some of the other disadvantages which children experience – working intensively on their academic skills, supporting the development of their language, offering them the places to play that are absent in the neighbourhood, and doing so within the contexts of local policies for creating a less disadvantaged mix of population in the area, and national policies to combat poverty and increase employment (ibid. chapter 5).

It is this latter, disadvantage-oriented rationale that has dominated much of the policy and advocacy literature on full service approaches. The Schools Plus report in England, for instance characterizes highly disadvantaged areas in much the same terms as Plowden. They are, it asserts, marked by three sets of problems:

- too many children in disadvantaged areas do not have access to the same range and quality of opportunities as those in more prosperous areas;
- some families in disadvantaged areas have difficulty in offering an appropriate level of learning support and encouragement to their children; and
- some children find that other factors – such as low family income or poor living conditions – affect their ability to participate fully in the opportunities available to others.

(DfEE, 1999, p. 14)

In this context, schools adopting extended approaches are expected to have important impacts: they are likely to generate 'high morale and standards leading to a cycle of success', and in turn 'attract[ing] supportive parents who value education'; they will foster partnership between teachers, parents and other 'stakeholders' in young people's education; their adult education provision will 'be a crucial factor in improving life chances and employability, as well as in raising parents' expectations for their children, and students' own expectations for themselves'; and they will act as 'a focal point – somewhere where people of all ages can meet' (DfEE, 1999, p. 16).

Similar rationales are evident in the USA. One of the most fully developed and thoughtful of these is offered by the Children's Aid Society (2001). At the heart of the rationale is an assertion that, as the skill and knowledge demands of the workplace increase, 'never before in our history has education been more vital to the future prospects of children' (Children's Aid Society, 2001, p. 22). At the same time, however, schools struggle to teach some young people even basic skills. This, the Society asserts (ibid. pp. 24–27), is because schools are struggling with 'new realities', which can be characterized under seven headings:

- persistent poverty;
- educational inequity, in which poor children have worse access to educational resources and opportunities than their peers;
- a widening achievement gap between minority and white students;
- changing family patterns, leaving many families are 'too overwhelmed to participate fully in their children's learning and development';
- inadequate community supports, leaving children unsupervised and unsafe in many neighbourhoods;

- changing demographics in relation to increasing immigration and a growing proportion of children who are English language learners; and
- concerns about school violence.

'Community' schools are conceptualized as a 'response' to these realities:

> today's community schools movement has grown out of a convergence of major shifts in the world that present new realities in the lives of children and families and new challenges to our public schools . . . Community schools are schools for today because they offer a comprehensive response to the needs of 21st Century children and their families.
>
> (ibid. p. 27)

The nature of that response is that such schools should:

> provid[e] students with extended learning opportunities, bringing together the key developmental influences in children's lives – families, communities and schools – and providing essential supports, protection, guidance and opportunities, community schools are designed to help all students develop into productive adults who are able to earn a decent living, become responsible family members, and contribute to the larger society through good citizenship.
>
> (ibid. p. 27)

The essential structure of this rationale is clear. It is not too different from that offered by Plowden's view of disadvantaged communities some 30 years earlier, or by the Schools Plus report (DfEE, 1999) at about the same time, or by many other advocacy and guidance documents in recent years. Expressed in the form of a theory of change, it presents:

- *A starting situation* in which education matters as a pathway to a successful life, but educational success depends on more than just schools. Communities and, especially, families also play a vital part. Problems arise because, in a changing society, the capacity of communities and families to play their part is under threat; communities fragment and struggle with social and economic problems, and families find themselves too 'overwhelmed' or too disconnected from education to help. As a result, children and young people lack the 'supports' they need to do well educationally, and schools struggle to teach them effectively.
- *A set of actions* which involve replicating the conditions of supportive communities and families by building services and learning opportunities into the school and (perhaps) working with parents and communities to build their capacity to support children.
- *A set of outcomes* in terms of educational success and social development for children and young people which will in turn see them emerge as 'productive adults'.

This kind of rationale has been so dominant in the development of full service and extended school approaches that it is easy to assume that it is the only one available. However, Plowden's more positive view of the community school as fostering virtuous circles indicates that there may be an alternative. The distinction Plowden draws between the situation facing most schools and that facing schools in highly disadvantaged areas is also significant. It is perhaps in the full service and extended school initiatives that have not been dominated by concerns about contemporary urban breakdown that alternatives become clearer. For instance, as we saw in the previous chapter, the earliest large-scale development of full service and extended approaches in England was in the form of the Cambridgeshire Village Colleges. Henry Morris's rationale for these bears repeating – not least because the colleges themselves continue to thrive to this day. Morris, readers will recall, was concerned about the drift of the rural population towards the towns because only there could they find the facilities they needed, along with employment and education and training opportunities. Although rural areas were relatively poor, what concerned him were threats to the sustainability of the rural way of life. He wanted his Village Colleges to consolidate and extend the community facilities that were available in rural settings as a means of retaining the population and enhancing their quality of life. In this way:

> The isolated and insulated school, which has now no organic connection with higher education, would form part of an institution in which the ultimate goal of education would be realized. As the community centre of the neighbourhood the village college would provide for the whole man, and abolish the duality of education and ordinary life. It would not only be the training ground for the art of living, but the place in which life is lived, the environment of a genuine corporate life. The dismal dispute of vocational and nonvocational education would not arise in it, because education and living would be equated. It would be a visible demonstration in stone of the continuity and never ceasingness of education.
>
> (Morris, 1924, p. XV)

If we think of Morris's rationale in terms of its implicit theory of change, the differences from later, disadvantage-focused articulations of the purposes of full service approaches become clear. In terms of the starting situation, Morris's attention is not so much on the impacts of intense urban poverty, but on the lack of proper facilities for rural people and communities. There seems to be no implication, therefore, that those people and communities are beset by social breakdown, or that children in those communities are incapable of learning until their personal and family dysfunctions are addressed. It follows that, although the actions envisaged by Morris are, like those of the Schools Plus report or the Children's Aid Society, about bringing activities and services together in one place, they are not primarily about building a set of 'supports' for people who will otherwise collapse. On the contrary, Morris writes about making the College a home for the local Scouts and Guides, a place where the Village Council and Allotment Holders' Association could meet, a venue for concerts, and a place where sports clubs could meet and play, as well as a place offering school and adult education. In other words, the focus is on providing opportunities rather than support. Not surprisingly, then, the outcomes that are envisaged are more about rural people living richer and more fulfilled lives than simply about avoiding 'social exclusion' or remaining in the dysfunctional grip of chaotic neighbourhoods.

In fact, it is not necessary to go so far back in history to find alternatives of this kind. The Canadian province of Saskatchewan has, in recent years, been developing a form of full service approach for its schools that it describes as 'SchoolPLUS' (Government of Saskatchewan, no date). The original rationale for this initiative has many familiar elements – an assertion that there are 'tectonic factors' shaking the foundations of traditional schooling, that these include poverty and its associated social stresses, that schools and human services operating separately from each other cannot cope with these problems, and that a new form of service organization bringing the two together is the most effective way of responding to these complex challenges (M Tymchak [chair] Task Force and Public Dialogue on the Role of the School, 2001). However, the analysis of the starting situation is not quite identical with that of the examples we cited earlier. As in Cambridgeshire, rural depopulation is seen as an important issue (ibid. p. 16). So too, however, are 'cross-cultural issues and opportunities' (ibid. p. 14) and, particularly, the social and educational position of First Nations people. Indeed, the picture which emerges is not one of inevitable social breakdown which schools have to solve. Rather, it is one in which the shifting of the 'tectonic plates' of society should be seen:

> not so much as disruptions as occasions and opportunities. At the risk of thoroughly mixing metaphors, we want to move from earthquakes to journeys. And journeys have critical moments that, ultimately, prove to be decisive for the future. We call these moments turning points.
>
> (ibid. pp. 25–26)

On the basis of this analysis, the reconstruction of public education envisioned by SchoolPLUS has outcomes that are not simply about supporting children in chaotic neighbourhoods and families. Instead, what is intended is:

> nothing more and nothing less than the forging of a new society . . . [which] may not feature the most dazzling of economies by national standards – in any case such measures mean very little compared with truly human values – but it can be a beautiful place to live, a land where the sun shines and the rivers flow. It can, above many other things, also be a good place to raise and educate children.
>
> (M Tymchak [chair] Task Force and Public Dialogue on the Role of the School, 2001, p. 25)

Not surprisingly, the actions embodied in SchoolPLUS are not entirely identical to those in approaches targeted exclusively at areas of disadvantage. One major difference is that the 'community school philosophy' embodied in SchoolPLUS is expected to be embraced by all schools and not just those serving 'at risk' students (ibid.

p. 47). Another is that SchoolPLUS is indeed based on a 'philosophy'. In other words, provision is driven not so much by the assumed effectiveness of bringing services together in one place, nor by the evident needs of particular communities and places, but by a set of underpinning 'values, beliefs and goals'. The resulting specification for a SchoolPLUS school is worth quoting at length. It is:

- A school that views itself as an integral part of the community;
- A school that views the whole community, its agencies, organizations, businesses, trades, churches, and so on, as a resource for the school;
- A school in which parents are valued as partners in the education of their children; where every effort is made to give them meaningful involvement in establishing the goals of the school and in the design of the educational program;
- A school in which the culture of the children and the culture of their community is strongly reflected in the school;
- A school in which a sincere effort is made to adapt the educational program to the needs of the children, to give them an optimal opportunity for success;
- A school that takes a developmental rather than a deficit approach to children; that begins where the child is and endeavors to take the child as far along the path of learning as possible;
- A school in which pupil consultation at all levels, but especially at the middle years and high school levels, is an important consideration in the determination of school policy and practice;
- A school that views its facilities as a resource for the community and seeks to find ways to share this resource under appropriate supervisory conditions.

(ibid. pp. 47–48)

What is particularly striking about this values-led specification is the distinctive relationship that is envisaged between the school on the one hand, and students, parents and community on the other. There is little sense here of chaotic communities, dysfunctional families, and disengaged young people who have to be saved by the combined forces of the school and its allied services. On the contrary, what seems to be intended is a balanced, mutually respectful relationship, in which parents are seen as 'partners' in the educational process, schools and communities are resources for each other, cultural diversity is respected, and students have a role in shaping the school in which they are educated. In other words, the 'new society' that is the intended outcome of SchoolPLUS is embodied in the practices of the school. Realizing these values in practice is, of course, likely to be anything but straightforward (see, for instance, Salm, 2007, 2009). From our point of view, however, what matters is that the Saskatchewan 'model' is underpinned by a theory of change very different from those that have become familiar in recent years from the bulk of US and UK literature.

School-level rationales

Whilst these initiative-level rationales offer a broad framework within which full service and extended schools can develop, our work with schools leads us to agree with Dryfoos' assertion that, 'in reality no two schools are alike; they are all different' (Dryfoos, 2005, p. vii). The semi-implicit nature of the theories of change underpinning most initiatives, the need for schools to respond to their individual circumstances, and the views and values of those leading work at the school level mean that they interpret their roles in very different ways. Whilst, therefore, it is important to examine rationales at the initiative level, if we really want to understand the assumptions which are embedded in full service and extended approaches, and the possibilities for conceptualizing these approaches differently, we must also look at what is happening at the school level.

In the course of our work, we have engaged with scores of schools – not to mention school clusters and local authorities – to surface the theories of change underpinning their efforts. Over time, the diversity of these theories has begun to reveal some stable patterns in terms of the assumptions on which schools build their work, and the choices their leaders make about how to operationalize their full service and extended school approaches. There are three issues in particular around which these assumptions and choices cohere:

- how the starting situation is framed, and therefore the kinds of outcomes that are intended;
- how the scope of school actions is conceptualized; and
- how the politics of the approach are understood.

We will consider each of these in turn.

Framing the situation

As we saw in looking at policy and guidance texts, full service and extended school approaches imply – and often make explicit – some understanding of the situations in which they are based, and therefore of the kinds of changes in those situations which the approach is seeking to make. The same is true of the accounts offered at school level. In our experience, when school leaders explain the rationale for their full service approaches, they frequently begin with a recital of the problems in the area served by the school. Typically, this is in terms of levels of poverty, educational (under-)performance, and social difficulties. The following is a typical example, taken from our fieldnotes in the Full Service Extended School Initiative:

> only 6% of young people achieved A*-C grades at GCSE and around 20% left without any qualifications. There were issues in the area around poverty (over 70% of school students were entitled to free school meals), health (male life expectancy was just 51 years), poor housing, debt, domestic violence, teenage

pregnancy, prostitution and drugs. Not only was unemployment in the area high, but some 90% of people in employment were women, with men unwilling or unable to take on such job opportunities as were available. The ward served by the school was in the 1% of most disadvantaged wards in the country. As the head put it: 'Lack of entitlement just stood out like a sore thumb across the community'.

(Cummings *et al.*, 2005, p. 128)

Framing the situation in this way implies that the development of a full service and extended school approach is a way of responding to these problems. As the head quoted above went on to explain:

We had to do something to try and raise attainment within school. There was no point in working in isolation because I think the temptation would be to close the doors, try and deal with all the major problems privately, because it is very risky in terms of PR to open up to the community and tell them what your problems are. But we decided to take the risk and go the other way round and open all the doors up and say, 'Okay, as a community, this is our school, how are we going to sort it out?' And that's really where the extended school concept started from.

(ibid. p. 129)

The details of analyses such as these vary, of course, from school to school. In some multi-ethnic areas, for instance relationships between different ethnic groups are seen as a major issue which schools have to address. In other areas, schools see themselves as dealing not so much with poverty and worklessness, as with poor-quality employment and the limited horizons of local people. Beneath these differences, however, the fundamental framing remains the same – the situation contains problems to which the full service and extended provision made by the school is, in part at least, the solution.

All of this, of course, echoes the sorts of analyses and rationales that we saw offered by Plowden, Schools Plus and the Children's Aid Society. However, this is not the only way in which situations can be framed. Occasionally, we come across schools developing full service and extended approaches in contexts where there are seen to be few if any social and educational problems. In one study (Dyson *et al.*, 2002), for instance, we worked with schools serving relatively advantaged areas where children did well educationally, and such deprivation as there might be was confined to 'pockets' here and there. Here, the emphasis was less on problems to be solved than on opportunities to be seized:

The rationale for [the school's approach] that was explained to us centred around a culture of life-long learning and a sense across the community that this is 'our school' (evidenced, for instance, through low levels of vandalism and graffiti). Impacts of extended school approaches were articulated in terms of benefits to children wider than the standards agenda. This includes respect of children and adults of varying ages as they all meet in and use the school, breaking down fear and ignorance of each other. This is shown particularly in children's calm behaviour in corridors where they might easily come across frail or disabled adults.

(Dyson *et al.*, 2002, p. 15)

Or, in another school:

The rationale . . . focuses on the school as a community resource – 'This is the community's [school] . . . not my school, not the teachers' school' (head). There is a view that this is 'a comprehensive school' and that 'people who live in the area are entitled to come here and it is our responsibility to provide an appropriate curriculum' (head).

(ibid. p. 19)

In cases such as this, there is undoubtedly something that schools can add to the situation they face, but doing so does not necessarily imply that this situation is understood solely in terms of the problems it contains. To that extent, we are reminded of the Saskatchewan formulation that the current state of society is characterized not by 'disruptions' so much as by 'occasions and opportunities'.

Conceptualizing scope

Full service and extended school approaches, as we argued in chapter one, understand children and their schools as located in wider family and community contexts. One issue to be resolved in formulating rationales for such approaches, therefore, is how far schools can and should intervene not just in children's learning, but also in the dynamics of families and communities. These decisions then shape what we call the 'scope' of the approach.

This issue is particularly salient for schools serving highly disadvantaged areas, where school leaders often feel that they cannot rely on families and communities to offer children effective support. In extreme – though not entirely atypical – cases, they may see this as an argument against engaging with families and communities at all, and restricting any extended services they offer to students. As one head teacher told us:

The school aims to provide a different sort of area for pupils in which it imposes a strict uniform and discipline code . . . The school is a safe haven and provides an alternative to the community . . . The number one priority is raising attainment as that is what it is accountable for . . . the priority is to teach pupils to read so that they can get their exams and leave [the area], so they can get out of there.

(Cummings and Dyson, 2007, p. 11)

More commonly, leaders of schools with full service approaches regard this as a non-viable strategy on the grounds that it is simply not possible (even if it is desirable) to insulate children from family and social influences. A better strategy is to engage with families and communities so that they are able to support the child's learning. As another head teacher put it: 'whilst the prime role of school is to educate, it is not going to be possible to drive up attainment without engaging fully with the community' (Cummings and Dyson, 2007, p. 11). However, although this ensures that the scope of the school's work will be wider, it still begs the question of just how far schools should 'extend' themselves. In one study, for instance, we encountered a school that was clear that the disadvantages besetting families and communities impacted negatively on children, but also felt that it should concentrate on what it knew best, offering educational opportunities to the community but not trying to solve a whole range of social problems (Dyson *et al.*, 2002, 17ff). Elsewhere, however, school leaders embark on very ambitious programmes, aimed at transforming the fundamental characteristics of local communities. As one told us:

> One of the things that we're going to have to look at through this is how we change the culture of the whole community . . . I want them to have different aspirations than they had when I came here [as head] – I think it'll take another generation for that bulk of people to actually change it for their children. So it is this long-term change that will make this biggest impact . . . If there are these small pockets that seem to be intractable then it's going to be long-term policies and long-term changes that'll change them rather than the short term.
>
> (Cummings *et al.*, 2007b, p. 194)

It is worth adding that scope in this sense is not simply about the range of school's actions, but also about the intended beneficiaries of the full service approach. In many cases, school leaders see even their widest-ranging actions in relation to benefits for children and, typically, improvements in their educational achievements and life chances. Even when transforming whole communities, the aim, ultimately, is to 'change it for children'. However, others adopt what elsewhere we have called a 'holistic focus' (Cummings *et al.*, 2007a, 26ff). In other words, they see children's learning and well-being as inextricable from the well-being of families and communities. At the same time, they see the well-being of families and communities as important in their own right, and so are prepared to offer services and activities even if it is difficult to see how children themselves might benefit.

The politics of the approach

It is not usual to see full service and extended school approaches as overtly political. For the most part, school personnel and leaders of initiatives at local and national level tend to present themselves (and doubtless see themselves) as acting benevolently in the evident best interests of children, families and communities. However, as we saw in chapter one, full service and extended approaches rise, and fall or are redefined, in line with the formal politics of education policy-making. Moreover, the differences of perspective we have identified throughout this chapter suggest that the 'best interests' of disadvantaged groups may not be nearly so self-evident as at first they appear. Neither is there any reason to assume that the interests of all supposed beneficiaries from full service and extended school approaches coincide in every case, let alone that they coincide with the interests of schools or policy makers. Since such approaches involve making choices about which interests will take priority, how different interests are defined, and who will get to do the defining, they are, in fact, intensely political.

In England, for instance, the lack of specificity in some aspects of national guidance means that, in practice, school leaders – and, in particular, the head teacher – have tended to dominate the decision-making process about what schools will and will not do. Indeed, the entire orientation of the school towards families and communities can be reversed by a change of head teacher (Cummings and Dyson, 2007). In turn, this means that the interest of children, families and communities come to be defined by the heads and other professionals in and around the school (Cummings *et al.*, 2007b). As work we have recently undertaken on how schools define and target disadvantaged groups suggests (Cummings *et al.*, 2010), the involvement of these supposed beneficiaries in articulating their own wishes and interests tends to be restricted to responding to consumer-survey type consultations. When it comes to understanding the children, and adults they serve, and deciding what it is they 'need', schools rely heavily on what front-line teachers and support workers say rather than on any direct involvement of local people themselves.

This may go some way to explaining the characterizations of children, families and communities that we are commonly offered by schools. We often find that they take the short step from describing the problems which beset children, families and communities to locating the source of those problems within those who experience them. The following, for instance, come from accounts offered by head teachers (cited in (Cummings *et al.*, 2007b):

> In general, pupils from [name of area] have very low aspirations. Very few aim for or get to university. Education is not seen as a priority.
> There is a very high risk of some male pupils turning to crime and some female pupils falling pregnant before they complete their education . . . Peer group pressure is an enormous influencing factor, as is family life.
> We have third generational unemployment and we need people to realize that there are some opportunities. We must help them to help themselves. Also there are lots of pressures on children; lots of drugs, crime and lack of work opportunities. We must get children into nursery and get parents in at that point and keep them on board, give them parenting skills.

Typically, as here, the material and social problems facing children and families are acknowledged, but local people are seen as contributing to their own downfall through their low aspirations, failure to pursue opportunities, susceptibility to peer pressure, and unsupportive family life. The implication is that if the school is to help solve the problems of the area, it somehow has to change the people who live there. In the words of the head teacher we quoted earlier, it becomes necessary to 'change the culture of the whole community'.

To some extent, this line of thinking is an understandable outcome where schools serve highly disadvantaged areas and many of their students face significant problems. There are alternatives, however. Not surprisingly, in the schools serving more affluent areas, the emphasis is less on saving local people from themselves, and more on developing shared values of respect and handing the school over to the community as 'their' resource. However, this is not simply a matter of where schools are located. Even schools serving disadvantaged areas can develop different views about the children and adults they serve, and about who gets to make decisions. The key seems to be in how school leaders respond to the evident need for them to 'help them help themselves'. One interpretation of this is that people are helpless until the school helps them change. Another is that people may need help in the face of overwhelming problems, but that this help should take the form of building their capacity to solve problems for themselves.

There are relatively few examples of this kind amongst the schools we have worked with – but there are enough to show that it is a realistic possibility. In the Full Service and Extended Schools initiative (Cummings *et al.*, 2007a, p. 28), for instance, some schools tried to develop students' leadership skills so that they could ultimately become community leaders, or invested in adult learning because they saw local people as potential 'achievers' if only they had the chance, or offered support to local people to become community activists. Likewise, we are currently working with a school which is sponsored by a social housing association (i.e. a provider of affordable housing). We shall say more about this school – 'Weston Academy' – in chapter seven. Suffice it to say now that the sponsor brings a much less school-centric perspective to the development of a full service approach, and one in which local people are seen as customers (with choices) and community members (with rights) rather than simply as more and less effective carers for children. As a result, the school has a focus not only on solving problems for children and families, but also getting students involved in community projects so that they build a sense of pride in the locality, and developing their skills as entrepreneurs so that they can develop new kinds of employment in the area. In these small ways, the balance perhaps tips from 'helping people' to 'helping people help themselves'.

So, what is a full service approach for?

In the previous chapter, we argued that there was no blueprint for full service and extended schools, and that instead we should think of a broad 'approach' which took different forms in different times and places. What we have seen in this chapter is that, in the same way, there is no single rationale for such an approach. Different initiatives seem to conceptualize the aims and characteristics of full service approaches in different ways. In some cases – as in England – questions of underlying rationale tend to be confined to the background whilst the practicalities of the services and activities to be offered receive most attention. In any case, individual schools are likely to develop their own more or less explicit rationales to reflect their own circumstances as they see them.

We have argued that it is important to surface these rationales so that fundamental assumptions about purpose and *modus operandi* do not get lost. A useful way to start this process is by asking how the situations are framed in which full service and extended schools are located, what outcomes are intended in those situations, and what actions are seen as likely to produce those outcomes. In this way, we can begin to surface underpinning theories of change and so interrogate the clusters of assumptions and choices on which they are based. When we do so, we find three such clusters – around the framing of the situation, the scope of action and the politics of the approach.

What emerges from the different examples we have considered in this chapter is that there is one rationale which is so dominant that, as we suggested earlier, it is tempting to see it as *the* rationale for full service approaches. At the very beginning of what we might call the 'modern' full service and extended school movement, Joy Dryfoos argued for the necessity of such schools in urban USA, on the grounds that:

> schools are failing because they cannot meet the complex needs of today's students . . . The cumulative effects of poverty have created social environments that challenge educators, community leaders, and practitioners of health, mental health, and social services to invent new kinds of institutional responses.
>
> (Dryfoos, 1994, p. xvii)

This captures the dominant rationale as well as anything – the sense that the social fabric in poor urban environments is disintegrating; that children and young people are the victims of this disintegration; that traditional forms of service delivery cannot cope and that schools are left dealing with the consequences; that new kinds of service configurations in and around schools are needed; and that these configurations will repair the damage that has been done to communities and families, and will thus enable children to learn and develop in productive ways.

Expressed in this way, the power of this rationale, and the appeal of full service and extended school approaches to policy makers and practitioners in many places is apparent. Unlike most other services, schools cannot ration what they offer, and cannot therefore avoid being overwhelmed by apparently growing social problems. On the other hand, they represent a major public investment in disadvantaged areas and have, deeply embedded in their roles, the aim of leading children and young people to a better life. Configuring services in and around them offers the prospect that they can overcome the challenges they face and accomplish their purposes much more effectively. It seems to provide a practical means of addressing the problems of the most disadvantaged areas, and equalizing outcomes between them and more favoured places. At the same time, if all that is involved is service reconfiguration, it holds out the tantalizing prospect of achieving these worthy aims with little or no new investment.

At the same time, however, the questions to which this rationale gives rise begin to be apparent. Whilst it makes some kind of sense in relation to areas of urban disadvantage, is it equally applicable in rural areas, or in less disadvantaged places? If the analysis of social disintegration is accurate, what prospect is there that schools – even with additional services – can reverse the process? How, precisely, will full service and extended schools make poor areas rich, or dysfunctional communities functional, or chaotic families supportive? Finally, how robust is that analysis? Can disadvantaged areas be understood solely in terms of their problems and the problematic behaviours and cultures of the people who live in them? Is it necessarily in the best interest of those people to have decisions about their lives made by professionals who claim to know best? And are school leaders, with their focus on children and children's educational achievements, necessarily the best people to lead interventions for families and communities as a whole?

These are questions to which we shall return later in this book. In the meantime, however, our analysis has also shown that there is an alternative – or, more accurately, alternatives – to the dominant rationale. Such alternatives are less common and less consensual. They have also been developed largely (though not exclusively) in relation to areas that are less hard-pressed than many urban environments. If the transferability of the dominant rationale to non-urban places is problematic, then questions must also be asked about how these alternatives might survive in harsher urban environments.

Nonetheless, it is clear that full service and extended school approaches need not be based on the assumption that the places where they are located are characterized by massive social problems. They might be places that are problem free, or where social change presents demands and opportunities, but is not necessarily overwhelming. The aim of schools, therefore, might be to enrich people's lives rather than to solve their problems. The ultimate outcome, moreover, may not be the equalization of more and less disadvantaged areas, but the development of a society based on 'human values'. In the same way, it is not necessarily the case that, even where people are facing problems, they have to be seen as helpless, and therefore dependent on the support of the school. Maybe schools can focus on developing the capacities of individuals and families rather than on solving their problems and changing their cultures. Maybe, therefore, local people can be involved in making decisions about schools, rather than schools taking decisions about local people. And perhaps full service and extended schools can contribute to the development of communities and societies as a whole, rather than focusing simply on 'saving' vulnerable children.

The existence of these alternative possibilities is important if we are to avoid the assumption that there is only one way for full service and extended school approaches to be understood. We will, therefore, return to their implications in due course. In the next chapter, however, we turn our attention from the rationales underpinning these approaches to a more detailed examination of one initiative in action. That is the Full Service Extended Schools initiative in England which began in 2003, and which we evaluated on behalf of the government ministry responsible for education – then known as the Department for Education and Skills.

Chapter 3

Inside the schools

In the first two chapters, we reviewed some of the history and international scope of full service and extended school initiatives, and examined the range of rationales that have underpinned approaches of this type. In the next four chapters, we wish to focus on one recent initiative – the 'Full Service Extended Schools' (FSES) initiative in England. There are a number of reasons for choosing this initiative. Pragmatically, this is one of a number of English initiatives that we have evaluated and where, as a result, we have detailed information on practices, processes, and outcomes. In the case of the FSES initiative, the evaluation was relatively generously resourced and relatively long-term (three years in total), meaning that we were able to undertake a study that was more robust than many in this field.

However, there are two other reasons for focusing on the FSES initiative. The first is that FSESs fall squarely within the mainstream of full service and extended school approaches, located as they were in areas of significant disadvantage, and with the aim of developing new forms of service delivery to meet the evident needs of children, families and communities in those areas. In broad terms, moreover, the basic assumptions on which they were founded and the major forms of provision they developed were not essentially different from English predecessors such as Plowden's community schools (Central Advisory Council for Education [England], 1967), nor from many of their international counterparts which we described in the previous two chapters. FSESs, therefore, take us to the heart of what most (though, of course, not all) such approaches have been like across the world.

The second reason is that FSESs were developed under particularly favourable conditions. Unusually in this field, they had the backing of central government rather than relying on local initiative or the intervention of charitable foundations. They were offered relatively generous levels of additional funding, together with the support of their local authorities and of a dedicated national support service – the Extended Schools Support Service. Moreover, although the additional funding itself was relatively short term, in many cases the schools which took advantage of it already had significant experience as providers of extended services, and well before the end of the FSES initiative that all schools would soon be required to offer such services (DfES, 2005b). The consequence has been that many of these schools have an unbroken history of full service provision from some time prior to 2003 up to the present day.

In this respect, the wider context in which FSESs developed is significant. As we saw in chapter one, FSESs were in no sense an isolated, one-off initiative. They built on a long history of full service and extended school provision in England, given added stimulus after 1997 by a series of smaller-scale extended school initiatives and by a policy focus on disadvantaged areas and populations. It is also worth remembering that, despite endless controversies about the quality of public services, it has long been an established principle of public policy in England that the state carries a responsibility for protecting its citizens from the worst effects of social and economic disadvantage. As the landmark Beveridge Report produced during the Second World War put it, the state's role is to tackle the five 'giants' of Want, Disease, Ignorance, Squalor and Idleness (Beveridge, 1942). As a result, FSESs and other similar initiatives have not needed to function as oases of support in deserts of service-deprivation. Instead, they have been able to work alongside relatively (in international terms) well-resourced, publicly led and publicly funded social care, health, welfare and other services. Under these circumstances, FSESs were well-placed to explore what could be achieved by new partnerships with and configurations of these services. Despite the undoubted challenges they faced, they were not constrained by the need to provide basic levels of support to the populations they served.

As we saw in earlier chapters, the FSES initiative proper ran from 2003 to 2006. The original focus was on promoting the development of one full service school serving an area of significant disadvantage in each local authority. Although there were the inevitable adjustments of direction and adaptations to fit local circumstances, by the end of the initiative some 150 schools were participating and most fulfilled the original expectations. By and large, these schools were volunteers, chosen through a process of negotiation between local authorities and individual schools. Sometimes local authorities had strategic aims in mind for selecting schools. For instance, one local authority we worked with was planning a radical transformation of all of its schools to make them service and community hubs, and used the FSES initiative to pilot this remodelling. Often, however, local authorities identified schools which had histories of extended provision, or which were particularly keen to be involved. As a result, most participating schools were willing volunteers, though with differing levels of experience in full service approaches.

Nationally, schools were offered guidance as to the sort of provision they were expected to make – community access to school facilities, adult learning opportunities, family support, study support, childcare, and stronger relationships with other child and family services. However, there was no central guidance as to how schools should configure this additional provision, what their precise aims should be, or how they should prioritize between different forms of provision. Individual schools, therefore, interpreted their remits in line with local circumstances and the views of their leaders, drawing on whatever support and guidance they could get from their local authorities and the national Extended Schools Support Service.

We noted in chapter one that FSESs received seed corn funding of up to £162,000 in the first year. This was more than enough for them to, say, employ a dedicated manager of their provision and make some activities and services available free of charge. However, for various reasons not all schools received the full amount, and in any case the funding declined each year and was only ever intended to provide a short-term stimulus. As a result, schools had to make considerable efforts to find additional funding (for instance, from charitable sources) and to secure the use of resources in kind (for instance, by persuading other services to allow their personnel to work from the school site). Most schools told us that they received between £200,000 and £400,000 in government funding over the lifetime of the project, and topped this up with no more than £100,000 of additional funding (Cummings *et al.*, 2007a, 92ff). However, when we made our own estimates of the financial value of the resources deployed in support of full service provision, the figures were much higher, reaching up to £2m per annum (ibid. 145ff).

In other words, the provision being made by schools was much more extensive than could have been supported by additional government funding, and relied heavily on using school staff time, personnel from other services, and voluntary inputs, for which no money needed to change hands. The implication of this, confirmed by our own fieldwork, was that, for many participating schools, the FSES initiative involved a major commitment on their part, with significant implications for how they used their resources and how they related to other agencies working in the areas they served. For some, indeed, it became central to the way they understood their roles and the way they set about their task as educators in areas of significant disadvantage.

In subsequent chapters, we will examine some of the challenges faced by these schools, the outcomes they achieved, and the way we set about identifying those outcomes. In the remainder of this chapter, however, we wish to go 'inside' FSESs, describing what we typically found when we explored their provision.

Inside the schools

What did FSESs look like?

Full service extended schools were (and in many cases still are) ordinary schools taking on an extra-ordinary role. As a result, their buildings were much like those of all other schools. At the start of the FSES initiative, a few were purpose-built or had had significant refurbishments or extensions. This became increasingly common subsequently as a major rebuilding of the school stock in England, known as 'Building Schools for the Future' (4ps & Partnership for Schools, 2008), took effect. Many, however, continued to be located in older buildings. Since some had experienced falling rolls as families sought out more 'desirable' schools in less hard-pressed areas, they often had spare accommodation which could be used to house their additional activities and services.

Externally, therefore, FSESs looked much the same as most other schools in England, apart, perhaps, from a reference to the extended provision on the school name board. Only internally did the differences become apparent. There might, for instance, be colourful notice boards in reception showcasing the extended provision on offer. In some cases, there was a separate entrance to a community wing or annex that was dedicated to this aspect of its work. Where schools were still in older buildings, they might have adapted vacant caretakers' houses, or refurbished a previously unused part of the school. Some made do with prefabricated huts located close to the main school building. In these dedicated areas, there would typically be a series of meeting rooms where some of the one-to-one support work took place, and perhaps community rooms equipped with soft furnishings and with small kitchens attached. There might be computer suites, and rooms assigned for the childcare or out of school hours provision. Almost invariably there was some office space for professionals from other agencies who were co-located in the school, or who came to the school to offer sessional provision. However, whilst some FSESs had new or refurbished rooms, others managed with whatever spare rooms or buildings they had available.

What did they aim to achieve?

The aims and foci of FSESs tended to reflect what they saw as the most pressing concerns and priorities in their own contexts. These differences in context could be significant. Some of the FSESs we studied, for instance, served predominantly white British areas, whilst others served multi-ethnic areas. Some were primary (age 5–11) whilst others were secondary (age 11–16 or 19) schools, and one was a special school for children with physical difficulties. Some were located in residential (usually, social housing) areas, with few local employment prospects but, equally, with little competition from other schools. Others were located in better connected areas, close to many businesses and industries, but also close to other schools who competed with them to recruit students.

The FSESs we worked with also, as we shall see shortly, had different interpretations of their roles within these different contexts. In the context of the national 'crusade for standards', they were all, of course, concerned with raising the attainments of their students. They all agreed that this meant working with the personal and social issues presented by their students, and, therefore, working with their families. However, they had different views about what, in the last chapter, we called the 'scope' of their approach – that is, about how far it was their responsibility to go beyond this by intervening in area-wide issues. They also differed in their understandings of the 'needs' of children, families and communities, in the point at which they thought they should intervene, and in the kinds of interventions they favoured. Despite these differences, however, it was commonly the case that schools saw users of their services primarily in terms of their 'problems'. Their task, as they understood it, was to save students, families and communities from the impoverished and dysfunctional lives that they might otherwise lead. There was widespread acknowledgement that, once the school had intervened, children and adults might become more stable, more productive and happier, but in only a few schools (one of which we describe later on) did we see any conviction that they already had the capacity to solve their own problems, or that they had attributes on which the school could build.

What did they do?

FSESs, as we saw earlier, were required to offer a number of forms of extended provision. However, they tended to interpret and prioritize these forms differently in line with their assessment of what was needed locally. This resulted in considerable variation in the services and activities that were on offer. For instance:

- Some schools made a substantial commitment to childcare provision as a way of enriching the lives and indirectly supporting the families of their students. They tended, therefore, to offer before and after school provision and extensive activities during the holidays. In a few (mainly primary) schools, crèche provision was also offered to enable parents of young children to access other FSES activities. Other schools, however, saw childcare as more of a matter for families themselves, and therefore made more limited provision to satisfy the requirements of the national guidance.
- In terms of adult learning, some schools regarded this as a priority and engaged a large number of community members in a wide range of classes. Others focused more on 'keeping up with the children' courses aimed at equipping parents to help with their children's school work. In some cases, adult education classes were accredited, whilst others were introductory or taster classes, aimed primarily at fuelling interest in learning and fostering self-esteem amongst those adults who had not studied for some time.
- Activities falling into the information and communications technology (ICT) strand typically included computer classes and community use of ICT suites, but there were also more innovative examples of students running and producing material for a school radio station, and producing CD ROMs on issues pertinent to them (such as bullying); and there were examples of inter-generational programmes involving students showing community members the basics of using computers.
- Whatever their view of childcare in general, most schools offered a wide and varied range of out of hours activities for their students. Here as much as anywhere, however, the different foci and different interpretations of the purpose of extended provision were apparent. Schools offered different combinations of homework clubs, breakfast clubs, learning mentor support, curriculum enrichment activities, sports activities, dance and drama festivals, arts activities, and many others. For some, the emphasis was on leisure and enrichment. For others, the emphasis was very firmly on extending the time available to support students' learning and work on raising their achievements.

What all of this points to is both the richness and diversity of FSESs' work, and the fundamental ambiguities as to underlying rationale which we explored in the previous chapter. All the schools were working within the same set of guidelines and the same funding regime, and most worked broadly within what we have called the 'dominant rationale' for full service and extended approaches. Yet they were in fact quite different from one another in respect of the activities and services they offered and the specific aims they hoped to achieve through their offer. If, therefore, we are to understand what FSESs did and why, we need to move beyond generalities and explore some individual schools in detail. It is to this task that we now turn. The case studies and references to particular schools and other institutions, and quotes from individuals have been anonymized. In all cases where names are used these are pseudonyms.

Three case studies of full service extended schools

Case 1: Beresford Primary School

The context

Beresford had been developing as an extended school since September 2000 when it was formed from the amalgamation of an infant and a junior school. The head teacher took the lead on these developments and had a clear vision of how it might provide a comprehensive package of support for students and families. However, she struggled to realize this vision in the face of limited external funding and resources, the absence of a regeneration strategy in the community, and a lack, as she saw it, of effective backing from the local authority.

Beresford is located in a pocket of disadvantage within a more affluent urban area. On the face of it, the area surrounding the school itself seems relatively affluent. In reality, however, Beresford serves two disadvantaged housing estates hidden within this more affluent area. As we have found in previous work (Clark *et al.*, 1999), small pockets of this kind tend to be invisible in area statistical indicators, and therefore miss out on the attention, resources and funding that their levels of disadvantage merit. In the case of the areas served by Beresford, lack of investment in the community, poor services and the absence of any effective regeneration efforts had left residents feeling somewhat neglected, and levels of community aspiration and self-esteem amongst children and families, we were told, were low. Families were experiencing health and social care difficulties that sometimes culminated in crisis situations, yet the structures in place to support these families were inadequate. As a result, the head teacher of Beresford estimated that she was spending up to 60 percent of her time attending to the non-educational problems besetting her students and their families.

The school first received government funding to develop as an FSES in 2002/03. This finally gave it the resources and external support to put the head teacher's plans into practice, and to begin developing more extensive collaborations with other services. Two main strands of action were put in place:

- The first was concerned with tackling the evident problems experienced by children and adults. This involved developing close relations with other agencies and enhancing the school's referral processes in the expectation that problems could be addressed early, before they had had chance to escalate. The assumption was that this would bring benefits in terms of children's learning and that levels of academic performance in the school (by which it would ultimately be judged) would in time improve.

• The second strand was focused on re-engaging parents and community members in learning, on the assumption that this would not only generate learning outcomes for them but also wider benefits such as raised levels of self-esteem and aspiration. Engagement in learning was also seen as bound up with 'empowering' local people, understood as being about enabling them to articulate their needs and take more control over their own lives. The assumption here was that the combination of learning and 'empowerment' would impact positively on aspiration and culture in the community and that this in turn would bring benefits in terms of learning and well-being for children in school.

Activities and services

Beresford created a family support team to offer rapid, proactive, integrated and non-threatening support to children and families. The team included the head teacher and assistant head teacher, a school-based social worker, FSES and childcare coordinators, counsellors from a local voluntary organization, a community support nurse, a parental engagement worker, a clinical psychologist from the Child and Adolescent Mental Health Services (CAMHS), tenancy support workers and a domestic violence worker. Some of these workers were funded by the school, but many (such as the counsellors, nurse and clinical psychologist) were not. However, the school offered all of them a base in an annex consisting of some prefabricated buildings. The intention was that a wide range of support should be on offer to children, families and the wider community, in a form that was readily accessible, holistic and capable of being tailored to the needs of particular users.

Configuring services in this way did not always mean that the ideal of early intervention could be achieved. In an area characterized by a relative paucity of service provision, professionals frequently found themselves engaged in reactive crisis management work. However, it was clear that the school's initiative was making more services available and was encouraging new ways of working. There had, for instance, been no social workers assigned specifically to the area, which meant that social work practice was inevitably somewhat reactive. However, the school-based social worker had the freedom to engage in preventative and non-formal work. Similarly, in the absence of any localized community health facilities before the initiative, the health provision on offer at Beresford filled a genuine gap. It was also evident that a collaborative model of working was beginning to emerge at the school. Joint strategy meetings were held, in which information was shared, assessments were made, decisions about appropriate involvement were reached, and intervention took place in a more coordinated manner than was usual in the local authority area.

The school also put its energies into developing provision that was open to all rather than being targeted at children and families in difficulties. A programme of adult learning was introduced, aimed at parents and other local residents, and a crèche was made available so that parents of young children could access the provision. A family learning programme was introduced, and the school's study support and out of school hours activities for students were open to all.

Impacts and outcomes

There was a good deal of positive evidence relating to the impacts of the family support team indicating that families did indeed feel better supported and more able to manage their problems, that children and adults began to engage in learning, and that the users of the school's services experienced increased levels of self-worth and confidence. The following account, adapted from our researcher's field notes, was given to us by a parent who had used the support offered by the school. 'Jenny' was typical of a number of women we met whose lives had been given a new direction by the work of an FSES. Like them, she had left school with few achievements to her name, had had children early, and had then spent her time looking after them. As a result, she had reached something of a dead end, with limited interests outside the home, no qualifications or work experience to enable her to move into employment, and little confidence in her ability to do more than she was already doing. However, as she told our researcher, the school changed things for her:

> Jenny has three children, one pre-school aged child, a daughter in Beresford and an older son at secondary school. She started a course at Beresford over a year ago when she heard through word of mouth that the school was going to start running courses for adults. She decided to attend after a member of staff gave her the encouragement to go along and because the venue was convenient for her. She also said:
>
> > It was easier doing the courses here as you knew some of the other parents already. I've also made more friends and this makes what you do easier. You don't worry about what you are doing.
>
> Jenny received the 'learner of the year award' in 2004 for her achievements in the adult learning sessions in school. She said:
>
> > I got the learner of the year award and I went bright red and wished the lights were lower but it really was a buzz. Everyone came up to me and said 'Well done, Jenny'.
>
> She has since gained the confidence to go to college once a week to do an art course and is continuing with the Maths and English courses which run at Beresford. Jenny said 'It gave me the confidence to go to college . . . I now feel excited and confident'.
>
> She has also started thinking about careers she might pursue. She is interested in writing children's books and illustrating the books herself. Recently she wrote a short story and the head teacher at the school is so impressed that she thinks that Jenny ought to try and get the book published . . . She has also suggested to Jenny that the school print the story and that it is read to the

children. This has made Jenny feel 'really proud' and motivated to devise new characters.

She decided she would like to write English books after starting the English course at Beresford (which she still attends) and although she might be dyslexic (the school are going to test for this) she has felt encouraged by the school to achieve her goal. She always knew she was good at art when she was at school but never pursued this and was never encouraged to do so by teachers in her school. The staff at Beresford, on the other hand, is very encouraging. The head teacher is keen to buy one of Jenny's paintings and is encouraging her to set up a stall at a local craft market to sell some of her paintings. Jenny thinks that the support and encouragement she is given is fantastic especially as she has been out of work for so long and did not feel confident about her abilities.

She attended a family learning course with her daughter and described the outcomes of the course for her daughter:

> Julie came in and took it all in when I did family literacy with her and her teachers said it gave her a lot more confidence in class to try new things rather than saying, 'I can't do it'. It's also improved her speech.

Jenny is also doing a first aid course at school also which, she says, is a 'useful qualification and a useful thing to know', and she attends the positive parenting classes because she wanted to learn more about dealing with teenagers and helping her 13 year old son who has attention deficit hyperactivity disorder (ADHD). She said:

> It was advertised and I wanted to go along to learn more. We went over problems parents face with teenagers and as I have a son with ADHD it helped a lot. I now think more about looking at things from their [teenagers'] points of view.

It seems clear that Jenny was more outward looking and more confident as a result of her engagement with the school. Indeed, at the time we spoke to her she was beginning to move beyond the relatively safe boundaries of the school by enrolling on a further education course and beginning to think about looking for employment. What seems particularly to have made the difference for her was the ongoing encouragement of staff who focused positively on her capabilities and recognized her achievements, and the availability of learning opportunities and support on her doorstep. Her story also suggests that Jenny's newly found self-belief, and her motivation to learn was beginning to impact on her daughter's confidence as a learner. The positive parenting classes may also have had an impact here. Jenny told us separately that these had led to her being able to receive counselling support for the domestic violence she had encountered in a previous relationship.

The school felt the cumulative impact of their work with adults like Jenny might ultimately make a difference at the level of the community as a whole. By the end of the FSES initiative, 48 families and 102 children had had some kind of formal support from the school and its services, and as many more had had informal support or had accessed childcare. In its own evaluation report, the school claimed that:

> the majority of families associated with the school have accessed extended provision via family support, lifelong learning or childcare. The work with the family support team has had a major impact on the lives of our children both within school and at home, with over a third of families on the school roll accessing support [in a single year].

The numbers of adults engaged in learning also pointed to relatively widespread impacts. By the end of the FSES initiative, 111 learners, including 69 parents of school students, achieved accredited qualifications, and, of these, nine had signed up to further courses at other centres. Similarly, 89 local families, including 58 families of children in school, were using the school's childcare facilities. In other words, in an area previously underserved by the statutory agencies, the school was beginning to reach significant numbers of local people, and it was likely that it would be even better placed to do so in future when a new children's centre opened on site. Although the dynamics of communities are difficult to predict, it is at least possible that, over time, the level of qualifications, confidence, and access to employment in the local community might change sufficiently to impact positively on local cultures and expectations.

There was, moreover, some evidence that the work of the school was bringing about these changes without making local people dependent on the services it provided. On the contrary, it seemed that the 'empowerment' aims of the school might indeed be starting to be realized. For instance, rather than the school having to target those they felt were 'needy', families were self-referring to the family support team and were signposting other community members to FSES provision. Some families and individuals who had engaged with the FSES provision were now attending community forums and meetings, where they were beginning to speak up for themselves on matters of local concern. Moreover, school leaders argued that their services and activities were having an impact on their 'core business' of raising levels of attainment amongst the student population. During the period of the FSES initiative, measured attainments rose significantly in the school. The head and her team were clear that this was due at least in part to the FSES provision, and particularly to the work of the family support team. In turn, this was, they felt, having an impact on the standing of the school in the local community.

Case 2: Clark Comprehensive School

The context

Clark is a comprehensive (i.e. non-selective) school for students aged 11+, serving a large, inner city, catchment area. It has suffered from a poor reputation and low levels of attainment in the past, though both of these were improving by the start of the FSES initiative. The local electoral district in which the school is located (its 'ward') is ranked within the top 10 per cent of most deprived wards nationally, and the community in which the school is based has, we were repeatedly told, historically been characterized by decline, neglect, low levels of aspiration and adults who have had a poor experience of education. When we spoke to school leaders, they told us that this situation was paralleled in the school, where many students displayed the signs of low self-esteem and low aspirations. Amongst these were some young people who encounter multiple personal and social problems which impact significantly on their learning.

The school had been developing full service and extended provision for several years. Much of its work was focused on providing its students with support to deal with their personal and social problems. It already had an 'inclusion' team to support, in particular, poor attendees, and hosted a multi-agency Behaviour and Educational Support (BEST) team, funded through the national Behaviour Improvement Programme (see Halsey *et al.*, 2005). It provided an 'alternative' curriculum for students who were struggling with the demands of more traditional academic work, offering a high degree of flexibility in what was learned and a high level of personalized learning support. The assumption was that this combination of services and activities, complemented by open-access enrichment activities outside of school hours, would re-engage students in learning, and increase levels of motivation, self-esteem and aspirations. In turn, this would impact positively on school performance. The school also wanted to develop its work with families to enable them to support their children more effectively, and to develop the use of school facilities as a community hub.

Activities and services

The on-site BEST team comprised a nurse, an 'emotional well-being' worker (social work trained), an 'inclusion' officer, learning mentors, family support worker and a joint coordinator for FSES and BEST. The team worked both in Clark itself and in feeder primaries whose students were likely to attend the school subsequently. The expectation was that this would make early intervention and preventative work easier to undertake, and would avoid the common pattern of problems being contained by primary schools only to burst into the open once the young person reaches the secondary school. The team, based in a new build at the entrance to the school site, was supplemented by a community police officer (who also had a room in the premises) and by a wide range of partner agencies based in the community. Members of the BEST team were allocated case loads which best reflected their own area of expertise, but in fact they rarely worked in isolation, tending to draw on the support of other professionals. They delivered one-to-one and group work on a range of issues including sexual health, weight management and self-esteem. They also involved families where appropriate, and had the capacity to refer swiftly to more specialized services if the need arose.

The school's alternative curriculum was provided off site, and there was also a student support centre on site offering personalized curriculum opportunities and learning mentor support. Non-targeted provision included a breakfast club and a school radio station, whose occasional broadcasts were planned and presented by students. There had also been a series of 'learning for life days' focused on a range of broader issues affecting children's lives, such as sexual health. In terms of community provision, there was a luncheon club for elderly residents, run by students following the alternative curriculum at a local community centre, and a senior citizens' club on the school premises. The school offered no adult learning provision at the time of the FSES initiative, but planned to do so in the future.

Impacts and outcomes

In our work with Clark, we assembled multiple accounts of how the school's provision had impacted positively on students and their families. There were examples where the close working relationships between professionals in and around the school had made it possible to undertake early intervention to prevent problems escalating, or, alternatively, where they had facilitated rapid access to specialist services where a situation had reached crisis point. Staff in the school also reported improved levels of confidence and self-esteem amongst students, which they felt went hand in hand with improved behaviour and engagement in learning. Students themselves spoke positively about the impact of the multi-professional team. Their responses when we asked them what would have happened had the school not set up this team were illuminating:

> I wouldn't be in school if it wasn't for BEST.
> I probably wouldn't come to school as much.
> If I didn't have it I wouldn't be able to cope. I got rejected from one school, but I don't think I would have coped there anyway cause they wouldn't have had the helping aspect . . . I wouldn't be here, I don't think I would be alive.

The alternative curriculum provision also received strong support from the students who experienced it. The following account is written by one such student, 'Simon', aged 15, who told the story of what happened after he had been excluded from other schools and education settings in the area:

> neither of these two placements [with other education providers] worked and the police were called because I was fighting and then I was asked to leave. At home I also started to get into trouble with the police. I had to attend court and had to attend Youth Offending Team sessions. I also started to use 'tac' [a drug] on a regular basis. Eventually I was allowed to go to Clark. However, within a short time I could not cope and started to fight, [be] aggressive to teachers and finally took drugs during school and ended up in hospital. During this time I was angry with everyone, teachers, pupils and people in general.
>   Last year I was asked if I would like to join the Alternative Curriculum programme . . . I had never heard of it but I thought I would give it a go. When I first

went there everyone made me feel so welcome. It's a small group, they seemed to like me and I was able to make friends. And the workers are mint, if you have a problem you can go to them and they'll help.

[*His first challenge came when he was asked to do some written work*]. I wrote something but I tossed it in the bin – I just panicked. But rather than being shouted at, the workers calmed me down. I thought everyone would laugh at me but instead they all helped me. This experience helped my confidence and I am now able to try new things without feeling afraid. Over the months my confidence has increased, I have achieved my bronze and silver ASDAN (Award Scheme Development and Accreditation Network) Award and am working on my gold (which I didn't think I would get). I have learnt how to cook, budget and run a lunch club for old people. I do writing and number work without getting aggressive and I am much calmer – that's not to say I don't still get angry, I am just learning how to cope with it better. I am also learning how to cope with people in authority better and I do outdoor education activities, which I really enjoy. I have made some good friends, learnt to trust adults and work together as a team to achieve goals . . . My relationship with my Mum has improved greatly (she is so proud of me now) and I have not been in trouble with the police in six months.

When we interviewed Simon, his mother, and his learning mentor, the same story emerged. His mother in particular spoke about how proud she was that her son was 'turning his life around' and paid credit to the work of the FSES, in particular the learning mentor at school and the youth support he received at the off-site centre. In her words: 'He has had all the support he will ever need'.

As with Beresford Primary, there were indications that these kinds of impacts were relatively widespread, at least amongst students. In the final year of the national FSES initiative, 20 students were accessing alternative curriculum provision. Over a period of one and a half school years, nearly 200 students – the majority of whom were students in feeder primary schools – received support from the BEST team. Participation rates were also collected for some of the open-access provision: during the first 14 weeks of delivery 32 students registered with the well-being clinic; the nurse reported seeing about eight students a week at the sexual health clinic; some 120 students accessed the breakfast club daily; 40–50 approximately attended an internet club; 32 took part in dance club; and 170 students accessed holiday activity days. The radio club attracted 145 student listeners and involved 64 students in planning and delivery in its first few days of broadcasting.

Levels of parental involvement were more difficult to gauge and the figures which were available suggested that relatively small numbers were taking part, leaving members of the school management feeling that they were simply 'scratching the surface' in terms of meeting the needs of vulnerable families. Moreover, only small numbers of community members made use of the school's provision. There was more encouraging evidence in relation to improved student attainment. Examination pass rates and performance in national tests rose, whilst absence and exclusion rates (schools in England can exclude students who present very serious disciplinary problems) declined. This last change in particular was dramatic. Some 86 exclusions took place in the year prior to the FSES initiative being launched, but only 15 in its final year.

Case study 3: St James' College

The context

St James' College educates secondary-aged young people and has developed special-isms in sports and in business and enterprise. It is located in a market town and serves a wide rural catchment. The school's standing in the community has improved in recent years but for a long time it suffered from a poor reputation. The area in which the school is based is characterized by socio-economic diversity with some areas of relative affluence and pockets of considerable disadvantage. This diversity is reflected in the performance of schools in the area. At the time of the FSES initiative, one of St James' feeder schools was the highest performing in the whole local authority; another was the lowest performing. The local population is stable with many parents of students having themselves been St James' students. However, the demography of the area is changing with the erection of some new homes and a growing Traveller community. There are relatively high rates of crime in some parts of the town, and community provision, in particular that for young people, is limited.

When we spoke to professionals in and around the College, they told us that many young people in the school experience emotional problems and have low self-esteem, both of which create barriers to learning. The College had, over the years, made efforts to address these problems through the development of an inclusion strategy and the creation of an inclusion team. Indeed, St James' had a history of community oriented schooling and had long since been designated as a community college with adult education and youth services on site. College leaders saw themselves as trying to promote social and educational 'inclusion', in order to improve young people's life chances. They anticipated that FSES developments would enable the College to build on existing community links and develop more robust support structures for vulnerable students and community members. In line with this rationale, two main strands of action were developed:

- The first focused on students. The College sought to develop its collaborations with other agencies in order to provide more effective support for students, both in the College itself and in its feeder primary schools. It also sought to develop a range of out-of-hours provision, aimed primarily at engaging young people in constructive activities before and after school and during the holidays. The expectation was that this would pay dividends in terms of developing students' skills, enjoyment and self-esteem. It was also hoped that the College's work with students would have wider impacts on the community, for instance by reducing levels of street crime.
- The second focused on families and community members. The College paral-leled its support for students with multi-agency support for vulnerable families

and community members. It also sought to encourage higher levels of parental involvement in their children's learning. The expectation was that this work would impact on levels of crime and ill-health in the area, but that it would also be reflected in school performance data and would contribute to the growing reputation of the College in the area.

Services and activities

The College developed strong links with statutory and voluntary agencies so that one-to-one and group support could be offered to the most 'needy' young people, families and community members. In order to co-locate services on the school site, a range of professionals – the childcare coordinator, education welfare officer, social worker, Connexions (careers) adviser, youth worker, youth justice worker and health worker – were given accommodation in a refurbished suite of rooms at the centre of the College building. Close working relations were also developed with many other public and voluntary agencies based off site, so that the College could signpost students and families to them whenever the need arose. In addition, the College worked with some of the more vulnerable students in feeder primary schools to try and intervene earlier in their problems. For instance, the youth justice worker and the youth issues officer from the local police force worked together to support and engage children who might subsequently be at risk of offending.

The College tried to give all students the opportunity to participate in activities outside the normal curriculum. The childcare coordinator expanded the range of out-of-hours provision on offer to young people. He has also recruited students as assistant leaders of these activities in order to build their skills and sense of responsibility. In the same way, the College established a student council to give students a voice in College policy, and young people were represented on the FSES steering group.

Adult learning activities had been offered on site in the recent past, but funding restrictions put a halt to this. The College intended to re-introduce them as part of its FSES provision. There were, however, some family learning and parent support groups, and some community use of the College's sports facilities.

Impacts and outcomes

As in Beresford and Clark Schools, we were offered many accounts of how the College's support provision had impacted positively on young people. College staff reported how the most vulnerable students were more settled in school, less disruptive in class, and achieved more highly. The young people corroborated these accounts, and some College students were particularly enthusiastic about how their encounters with the youth justice worker had helped them manage their problems – not least because, as part of the programme, they were mentoring children in local primary schools whose behaviour was causing concern. There was also a positive response from both staff and students to the open-access provision. Young people involved in the student council and FSES steering group, for instance, told us how they felt valued and listened to, and how the experience had helped to build their confidence. There was less evidence of impacts on parents. However, the parents we spoke with appreciated the support their children received and regarded positively the work the school was doing.

There was no evidence of large-scale impacts on overall levels of measured attainment in St James', though College leaders were confident that these would emerge in time. They were already able to identify particular vulnerable students who had achieved more highly than they would otherwise have done (indeed, some would have dropped out of school altogether) as a result of the interventions the College was able to marshal. There was, moreover, a decrease in the proportion of students leaving school with no qualifications and a reduction in student absences.

There was, however, some evidence that the College's extended provision was beginning to have an impact on some indicators of well-being in the area as a whole. As a member of the College's leadership team told us:

> The teenage pregnancy EWO [education welfare officer] phoned and said it's the first time we've not had a teenage pregnancy in your school and this is because of the pushing of sexual health [provision] . . . and child protection referrals have been zero since September. Also, the last [police] report of an assault in college was 18 months ago. This isn't to say they are not occurring but they are probably being dealt with more effectively in school.

The key factor underlying these impacts seems to have been the College's capacity to intervene early in student's problems and stop them escalating. As the police officer associated with the College put it, 'The school deals with things before things get out of order'. Interestingly, she also reported a knock-on effect in the 'improved reputation of the school'. Students also commented that the College's reputation was 'improving all the time' as a result of the extended provision that was being developed. A parent governor from the Traveller community felt that the school was 'a marvel' – something that is particularly noteworthy given that schools sometimes struggle to engage Traveller groups (DfES, 2005a).

Whilst St James' did not initially have ambitions to impact on the community as a whole, these impacts persuaded leaders that this might be within the realms of possibility. The College already had links with the town partnership (a coordinating body for organizations and services active in the area), the local children's centre, and the local area trust which led the town regeneration strategy. By the end of the FSES initiative, the College was developing plans to lead on the creation of a 'vision' for the town and a more formal partnership arrangement, which would focus on early intervention and the commissioning of services for children. The hope was that, alongside other benefits, this would eventually reduce the gap in attainment between young people from more and less favoured backgrounds.

Emerging themes

What is immediately striking about these full service extended schools is the enthusiasm with which they had embraced their new role, and the explosion of activity over a very short period of time. It is worth remembering that they had no detailed model to follow and there was no external agency able to set up their extended provision for them. Everything depended on the commitment and energy of school leaders. The disadvantages of this situation, in terms of the extra burden on these leaders, are obvious. However, there were balancing advantages, in terms of the integration of the schools' full service provision with their 'core business' of teaching and learning. In these schools, as in most other FSESs we worked with, services and activities were not simply bolted on to an otherwise unchanged school, but were seen as central to the way the school tackled inequalities in educational achievement, and to a wider social role through which the school contributed to the well-being of the communities it served.

It is also striking that this integration of the extended and core roles of the school seems to have enhanced their capacity to tackle issues that prevented children and young people learning. In these FSESs – as in schools everywhere – students were bringing with them into the classroom a whole range of personal and family problems. However, whereas most schools were limited in their responses to what they could do in the classroom and through somewhat minimal work with parents, the FSESs were able to trigger multi-strand interventions. In particular, they could complement their limited resources with those of the other service-providers with whom they had developed close working relationships, and who, in many cases, contributed to in-house multi-professional teams. Because schools could offer different forms of support and tackle multiple problems simultaneously, some of the delays in accessing provision and gaps in provision which beset traditional 'silo-based' forms of delivery seem to have been overcome. Perhaps not surprisingly, vulnerable individuals such as Jenny at Beresford or Simon at Clark found themselves receiving timely and sustained support which prevented problems escalating and seemed to shift their lives onto a different and more positive trajectory.

However, not everything was quite so positive. The integration of schools' extended and core roles inevitably meant that full service provision was shaped to a significant extent around their core concern with raising student achievement. Whatever other agendas drove provision at these three schools, the additional services they offered were invariably targeted at overcoming what were described as 'barriers to learning'. In itself, this was not necessarily problematic. No-one would deny that learning is important and that achievement in school opens up greater life chances. However, it was noticeable how in these schools, as in others in the FSES initiative, educational achievement became elided with measured attainment and then with the performance indicators by which the success of the school was measured. The distinction between acting in the best interests of the child and acting in the best interests of the school was, therefore, one that was constantly blurred.

There must also be doubts about the implications of focusing so much on 'barriers to learning' when a focus on 'barriers to health', or 'well-being', or 'relationships' might have uncovered different ways of working with young people, or, indeed, have revealed quite different groups who needed additional support and opportunities. As we have discovered in subsequent work (Cummings *et al.*, 2010), schools tend to rely heavily on their staff's uncorroborated perceptions of what their students 'need', rather than on a more formalized and searching investigation. Perhaps more important, the focus on 'barriers' of any kind inevitably locked these FSESs into the deficit and disadvantage perspective which, as we saw in the previous chapter, has tended to dominate this field. In all three schools, despite their very different area contexts, full service and extended provision was understood primarily as a means of tackling problems. These problems, moreover, seemed to relate to the failings of the children and adults who experienced them – students who failed to learn, families who failed to support their children, and communities where people had disengaged from the supposed mainstream values of work and lifelong learning.

And yet, this judgement may be too simplistic. What was also striking about these schools were the ambiguities, different interpretations and alternative possibilities which characterized their approaches to their full service and extended role. Beresford Primary, for instance, seemed to be developing an approach to the difficulties experienced by local people that cast them as part of the solution rather than as the source of the problem. Indeed, all three schools offered some form of open-access provision that was not targeted exclusively at 'disadvantaged' students, and seemed to offer enhanced experiences and opportunities rather than interventions in personal and family problems. If, therefore, much of the work of these schools could be understood in terms of the disadvantage- and deficit-focused rationales we examined in the previous chapter, at least some elements seemed closer to the focus on assets, opportunities and participation which we detected in the original visions of the Cambridgeshire Village Colleges or the Saskatchewan SchoolPLUS initiative. This ambiguity was typical of many FSESs.

Similar ambiguities are evident around what we have called here the different 'strands' of action in FSESs. If all three schools focused on 'needy' students, they also offered something to families and adults in the wider community. However, the emphasis they placed on these other strands, and the aims of their work with families and communities varied somewhat. Clark was perhaps most exclusively focused on the student agenda, with little evident activity in or impact on the wider community. St James' College was expanding into a wider community role, though it remained to be seen what its new proposal for 'town management' would mean in practice. Beresford Primary was perhaps most fully oriented towards family and community, but this raises questions about what work with adults might mean. The concern with 'engagement with learning' on which much of this work was based may indeed signal an issue that is important for the well-being of disadvantaged communities. However, it is also what one might expect to be the focus of interventions led by educationalists, and may or may not have matched the best interests of local residents themselves. At the same time, the school's characterization of its focus does not quite describe what it was doing in practice, in terms of the support it was giving to community activism or the marshalling of additional supportive resources in a service-poor area. There were, it seems, many directions in which Beresford's work might have developed, and the theory of change on which its work was based was not yet fully formed.

There were also ambiguities around the relationship between schools' full service and extended provision, the other child and family services that were provided in local communities, and wider strategies for tackling disadvantage in the areas served by the schools. The FSES initiative was based on a model of services and activities being located in and around individual schools. To some extent, as in the case of Beresford's school-based social worker, this simply meant that schools provided and managed services that were not being provided by other agencies. However, the fact that schools were not funded to make large-scale provision of this kind meant that, as in the three cases here, they relied heavily on inputs from other service providers. However, they did not control these other services, and typically found themselves locked more or less willingly into their agendas. So, we see the three schools here addressing issues such as teenage pregnancy, street crime, drug misuse, and adult (un)employment – none of which, strictly speaking, is an educational issue. Whilst, therefore, full service provision was, as we have argued, largely dominated by school concerns, there is also a sense in which school concerns were beginning to be broadened to include those of other agencies. Where this might lead we just begin to see in the case of St James' College. The partnership with the trust driving the regeneration strategy (the kind of partnership Beresford's head dearly wanted), and the emerging town partnership perhaps show the College shifting its role from that of a service hub to one of being a contributor to a coordinated network of provision and a coherent strategy for development of the area. The implications of this shift are, as we shall see later in this book, considerable.

These ambiguities and uncertainties neatly illustrate how much remains unresolved in the full service and extended schools agenda overall. It is not simply that there is no blueprint for how schools of this kind should operate, but that, as we suggested in earlier chapters, questions of fundamental purpose, of the framing of the social and educational problems they address, and of the nature of appropriate responses to those problems, remain somewhat open. Indeed, these cases raise many other issues than the ones we have outlined earlier. There is, for instance, the question of the ambiguous role of national policy – driving schools to focus on attainment on the one hand, yet offering them resources and supportive structures to take on a wider role on the other. There is also the vexed question of outcomes – the contrast between the significantly positive impacts on particular individuals and families and the somewhat weaker impacts on whole-school and community populations, not to mention the issue of the robustness of the evidence for these impacts. These, and all the other issues we have raised in this chapter, are ones to which we shall return in the remainder of this book. As a way of starting this process, we move on in the next chapter to consider the 'process' issues around FSESs – what made them 'work', what problems did they encounter, and what can other full service and extended school initiatives learn from them?

Chapter 4

Challenges and possibilities

In the previous chapter, we described how schools responded to being involved in the Full Service Extended School initiative in England – what forms of service and activities they provided, how they understood the purposes of that provision, and what kinds of impacts they had on children, families and communities. We also indicated that their responses were full of both ambiguities and possibilities, and that they raised a wide range of issues for full service and extended school approaches in other contexts. In this chapter, we want to explore some of those issues further. In particular, we want to consider what the implications might be of schools that are set up for one kind of purpose – teaching children and young people – developing additional forms of provision that are aimed at somewhat different purposes and targeted at groups other than their own students. As in the previous chapter, we will draw on our detailed findings from the evaluation of the FSES initiative in England. However, the issues we raise are not peculiar to that initiative and will, we believe, have resonance with full service and extended schools more generally, and in other parts of the world.

Management

As schools such as Beresford, Clark and St James' College developed their full service provision, they added a wide range of new activities, services, responsibilities and partnerships to their core business of teaching children. All of this new work needed to be managed and led in some way. So long as the new provision was limited in scope, head teachers were in fact able to manage it themselves, or to delegate responsibilities within their existing management structures. However, in most FSESs, provision was too extensive and complex to make this a viable option. This created a dilemma for heads who found themselves having to balance their responsibility for teaching and learning in the school with what seemed like an ever-increasing range of other duties. As one put it 'yes, the head will have a wider role, but their focus must be still very much about effective learning ... Maybe what we are looking at is a different configuration within senior management'.

This 'different configuration' took different forms, but most often involved creating a designated 'FSES coordinator' post, sometimes shared by more than one professional. These coordinators took from the head the responsibility for the day-to-day management of provision, forging community links, developing partnerships with other agencies and providers, and overseeing the school's strategic plans for extended provision. Finding some kind of workable structure brought a double benefit to head teachers. Not only were they freed from the burdens of managing provision on a day-to-day basis, but the provision itself freed them from the non-educational demands to which they had previously been subject. As Beresford's head teacher explained:

> I was finding, because of the nature of the community, when I looked at my role as a head teacher which is about leading the learning and the teaching, so much of my time was being taken up dealing with the social work issues . . . I did a review over a four week period of my time and 60 per cent of that time was social work related and that's not where my strengths are. My strengths are in teaching and learning.

Where schools opted for designated FSES coordinators, the role seemed to work best if it was adequately resourced in terms of time, and if it complemented any other leadership responsibilities the coordinator might have. Given that many coordinators did not have extensive leadership experience in schools, it also worked well if the head judged carefully what responsibilities they could be asked to take on, and if the role was located within a supportive school leadership structure. However, there were problems where coordinators had too little time or too many responsibilities. They could then feel themselves to be over-stretched and some of the burden would begin to fall back on head teachers. In the worst cases, there were examples of coordinators feeling 'vulnerable', 'isolated' and 'pressured' and being unsure where to prioritize their time and effort.

There was also the danger that a divide could open up between the school's full service provision and its core teaching and learning role. We occasionally encountered schools where the FSES coordinator effectively managed a separate operation which just happened to be located on the school site, whilst the head concentrated on leading the academic work of the school in a way that was largely unaffected by FSES status. The key to avoiding this seemed to be the continued engagement of the head teacher. In many schools, heads not only remained fully committed to full service provision, but their attitudes, drive and vision were fundamental to its development. Whilst they still needed an effective coordinator, they typically saw the development of the full service role as integral to the overall development of the school. Rather than academic achievement and full service provision being seen as separate domains, the latter was seen as a key contributor to the former. Where this happened, heads were likely to break down some of the traditional management silos which divided, for instance, responsibilities for academic work, pastoral work and special needs education between different individuals and sections of the school. FSES coordinators in these cases often became key members of the school's senior leadership team, working on an equal footing with leaders of the school's academic work, and perhaps took on responsibility for other related aspects of the school's work. St James' College, for instance, was one of a number of schools where the FSES coordinator was also the 'inclusion coordinator', responsible for the school's work with students with special educational needs and other difficulties.

Developing these kinds of management structures also meant in time that 'hero leadership' approaches had to be abandoned. Although the head's strategic involvement remained crucial, simple command and control from the top was impracticable. The FSES coordinator often became a powerful player in the school, with specialist knowledge of family and community issues that the head could not claim. The coordinator also developed a network of contacts beyond the school, and might in particular work closely with an FSES coordinator in the local authority. As partnerships with the local authority and with other agencies developed, decision-making about the development of provision increasingly began to involve these external partners. At best, this meant that the school became an outward-looking organization, locked into a network of provision in the area it served, and with the head and coordinator working closely together to ensure coherence across all of the school's activities. However, as these external networks became more extensive and complex, the danger once again arose that they would become a semi-autonomous 'empire', making little impact on what happened internally within the school. In at least one of the schools we worked with, this separation became so marked that the head felt the only solution was to replace the coordinator, dismantle the provision that had been built up, and start again. As she told us, the school was offering an impressive range of services and activities, but if you talked to most teachers, they would have no idea what was going on or how it related to their own work.

New workforce roles

Developing full service provision not only placed additional demands on management, but also called for personnel to deliver services and activities. Sometimes, this was achieved simply by teachers taking on new roles. However, the development of FSESs coincided with another government initiative on 'workforce remodeling' (DfES, 2002b). In essence, this effectively meant transferring as many non-teaching responsibilities as possible to other staff in school (often appointed for the purpose), so that teachers themselves could concentrate on the business of 'raising standards' in the classroom. Not surprisingly, in this context, both central government and individual head teachers were keen to ensure that running full service provision did not simply re-impose non-classroom duties on teachers. Instead, therefore, heads tended to staff their provision by calling on some combination of specially appointed non-teaching staff, and personnel from partner agencies and organizations. In combination with the workforce remodeling strategy as a whole, this meant that it was no longer only teachers who worked with schools' student bodies. Instead, the teachers were rapidly joined by a whole range of teaching assistants, learning mentors, family support workers, health workers, police officers, social workers and other non-teaching personnel.

This inevitably had implications for the work of teachers themselves. We have already referred to the 'pastoral' role which teachers in England have traditionally taken on in addition to their classroom-based 'academic' role. In other words, they have taken some responsibility for their students' welfare, for working with families, offering out-of-hours activities, and so on. Paradoxically, in some FSESs at least, as the range of services and activities offered by the school increased, the part played by teachers in making that offer decreased. The head of one secondary school, for instance, described what was happening to the 'heads of year' – the middle managers who had traditionally led the school's pastoral work:

> There are fundamental changes in the way we – or certainly I . . . see heads of year working in the future. There's a lot of fire-fighting; there's a lot of the discipline stuff. And we see that, hopefully, being removed from them, so they've got a more academic perspective on their children . . . as well as the pastoral side of things. But they spend most of their time now – or so it seems – fire-fighting . . . [S]omething that I'm quite interested in is having . . . a non-teaching year head. They're not a teacher – they do all of the attendance stuff; they do all of the behaviour stuff; they do weekly communications to form tutors about pupils who may be causing problems; they're always available to go out on visits with the year group. And then the head of year is then released to all the kind of academic . . . picking up on target-setting; seeing where people are falling off. So, their work needs to be more rooted in learning.

In many ways, this reconfiguration of roles was analogous to what was happening to some heads as FSES coordinators took over some of their 'non-academic' responsibilities. It carried, of course, the same danger – that a divide would open up between the classroom-focused work of teachers, and the work of a new contingent of non-teaching staff.

The advent of new types of school personnel also meant – again, somewhat paradoxically – that, as teachers became distanced from their pastoral roles, the school as a whole became a little more fully integrated into its community context. This is because many of the non-teaching staff who were brought into school were local people – perhaps even parents of students in the school. Some of them were employed precisely because they were expected to bring with them a knowledge of the area which teachers might not have. For instance, schools serving populations where English was not the first language might appoint local people who spoke one or more community languages and were able to win the trust of local people. There were also other kinds of cultural understanding that schools felt were important. One secondary school, for instance, introduced us to a non-teaching staff member who worked with some of the school's most troublesome students. It turned out that she was herself the mother of two such students, and had previously been involved in serious confrontations with staff in the school. Rather than rejecting her, however, the school had worked with her, won her confidence, and was now using her knowledge and skills to work with children not unlike her own. Recruiting local people in this way also meant that FSESs became players in the local labour market and in the development of adult skills in the area. As the head of one school explained:

> We grow our own and this all links to job opportunities and regeneration . . . [name of member of staff] is a community coordinator and a mentor. All the support staff with the exception of one are local people who start as volunteer helpers, dinner supervisors, classroom assistants and now high level teaching assistants . . . those people access employment as these are jobs that need to be done. They can also work within their benefit limits. They grow self-confidence.

A further implication of the reconfiguration of roles was that a range of roles that had traditionally been based outside the school in social care agencies, voluntary agencies, health organizations or the local education authority, were now undertaken by professionals who were employed directly by, or based for significant period of time in, the school. This meant in turn that new kinds of role began to appear in order to carry out the sorts of tasks that schools felt were important. This was particularly true of 'family support workers' (the job title varied). They worked with families, much as social workers have traditionally done, but their interventions were likely to be triggered at much lower levels of need, and by school-related issues, such as children's absenteeism or difficult behaviour. In general terms, the historically clear boundaries between schools and other agencies began to be blurred. Schools extended their work beyond narrowly academic activities on the grounds that this would contribute to the 'improvement of life chances' for their students, or 'help in tackling barriers to learning' and therefore assist in 'achieving the academic targets'. Other agencies similarly saw that they could undertake 'preventative work' and so meet their 'targets' more easily if they could access children and their families through schools. Given the target-driven nature of school and agency cultures, this created a win-win situation in which collaboration helped each professional group. As one FSES coordinator explained:

> The health service has targets around the number of young people who access medical provision. Well, we've set up a teenage health clinic and we've got more people accessing it which helps us support the young people here who wouldn't necessarily access the provision at the doctors surgery and at the same time health can almost tick that off in terms of targets they are hitting. It's about looking at a shared vision and unless you've got that shared vision how will it work?

This was not simply an instrumental way of meeting service targets. Both schools and their partners believed that working across professional and agency boundaries in this way delivered better services to their users. One social worker explained how this meant that, for the school she was 'more accessible' and had 'more ways of communicating with the area team if need be', and for parents she was readily available if they needed to talk. She also pointed to the 'less intimidating' environment for service users. Students, for example, might enjoy a level of confidentiality with an 'external' professional that might not be possible with teachers working in the school context – a view that was reiterated by a local authority officer:

It helps when things are run by people who are not teachers because the kids appreciate the confidentiality they are offered. They can discuss an issue with a nurse who isn't going to sit in front of them and teach them English the next lesson. That's a big benefit.

There were also perceived benefits in terms of mutual understanding between professionals. Working together could remove a blame culture that sometimes pervaded the interaction of different professional groups. As one head teacher explained 'We [the school and other agencies] are now talking together and have a greater understanding of what it is that we are all trying to do'.

There were, however, considerable challenges and unanswered issues. On the one hand, if they worked with staff from other agencies, they had little control over who these professionals were or how they operated. On the other hand, if they employed their own personnel directly, the fact that they had to call on 'non-core' budgets meant that they could often only offer short-term contracts, which in turn caused recruitment and retention problems. They then found themselves managing non-teaching professionals who had no effective professional support structures, were uncertain over promotion and identity, had to adapt to an unfamiliar working environment, and were asked to adopt working practices that were in conflict with their usual professional protocols. Child and family support workers could in particular find themselves working more or less alone in the most difficult of situations. In one school, for instance, the team manager for these workers was trained as a school administrator, and had no background in social or therapeutic work with families. Not surprisingly, these non-education professionals sometimes felt that the essential requirements of their role were simply misunderstood by schools. A sexual health worker, for instance, found that basic needs for confidentiality were overlooked in deciding where to place her office:

> There are some drawbacks to this particular location. The main one, which has come from the young people and staff, is that you have to come in from outside and it's exposed to the play yard and you don't want to access services if you are going to be seen. The original idea was for pupils to come in more discretely and have a connection from the main school into this building but the money ran out.

In many FSESs, practical problems of this kind were not fatal to the overall project of extending what could be provided on the school site. Schools and their partners in other agencies worked hard to tackle these practicalities and develop often impressive arrays of services. This could not be done in the short term, but over the three years of the initiative we saw schools where provision expanded, trust was built gradually, and managers across services became convinced of the benefits of working collaboratively. However, it is probably worth adding that the focus on practical issues meant that we saw few examples of criticality in thinking about the co-location of services in schools. The shared assumption seemed to be that students and their families had problems which either could not be dealt with efficiently or could not be dealt with at all by services as traditionally configured. Full service provision would give them quicker access to better services and at the same time would enable all the partners to meet their separate targets. Beyond this, we encountered very little discussion of how this might change professional roles, or the role of the school *vis à vis* other agencies, or what the agencies collectively were trying to achieve. These are essentially strategic questions, and strategy, as we shall now see, was a problematic issue for many FSESs.

Strategy

It was a relatively straightforward matter for FSESs to develop an outwardly impressive range of provision on an *ad hoc* basis – setting up services to meet some self-evident need, or seizing opportunities to put unrelated activities in place. It was much more challenging for them to work strategically, developing a clear rationale for their work and building services and activities coherently on the basis of that rationale. Partly, this was because many school leaders seemed to be more comfortable in making things happen than in spending time thinking about fundamental purposes. Partly, it was because schools had to pursue multiple sources of short-term funding in order to make their provision viable, and each funding source tended to have its own requirements in terms of aims and outcomes. Partly, too, it was because, as we saw earlier in this book, there is no single rationale on which full service and extended schools can be built, and, in the English context, government guidance itself tended to focus more on the what of full service provision rather than the why.

In these circumstances, it is not surprising that there was a tendency for schools to go their own way, determining their own purposes and calling on whatever resources they could lay their hands on locally. By and large, they found it difficult to get much help in developing coherent strategies, or in locating the work of their school in wider approaches to the development of the areas they served. In particular, they might have expected support from their local authorities. Not only do they carry responsibility for education strategy at local level but also for acting as 'place shapers' (Lyons, 2006), marshalling resources, services, and interventions strategically to support the development of the areas for which they are responsible. In practice, some support from local authorities was indeed forthcoming. In most cases, they were able to provide some practical guidance and some brokerage between schools and potential partners, which FSES leaders found very helpful. In a few cases, they were able to go beyond this. As we saw in chapter one, New Labour governments since 1997 had been much taken by the idea that the complex problems of disadvantaged places and people could only be solved through 'joined up' approaches. They therefore set in place a range of structures and processes for bringing services and organizations together within a single strategic framework – most notably through the Every Child Matters agenda (DfES, 2003a) for developing integrated services. As the FSES initiative unfolded, there were some places where this approach was beginning to produce an impressive array of coordinating mechanisms, so that the work of schools could be located within a wider area strategy. One local authority officer, for instance, explained how this strategy was embodied in, amongst other things, a 'joint area agreement' setting out agreed priorities and targets to be shared by a range of influential actors in the area:

> The joint agreement is at the highest level – Chief Executive level – and the senior managers under the Chief Exec are totally supportive, then everything else falls into place. So it is a clarity of mandate for multiagency working and currently we have that at Government level, across the different offices – you know, the Home Office, DfES, Health Department . . . and at the authority-wide level where structures are in place in order to support this networking in the mandate – the Chief Executives meet, they also have a joint agreement for this way of working including pooled budgets, they have a health group at the C[hief] E[xecutive] level which is also looking at shared targets and delivery . . . But the PCT [Primary Care Trust] is the biggest partner, and then obviously we have the NHS [National Health Service] care trust, and then the Police which are perceived to be part of the local authority.

There were indeed places where, out of structures such as these, emerged a clear strategy which FSESs understood and to which they could contribute. However, it is not too difficult to see how the complex system of 'joining up' different services and organizations could easily become bureaucratic and work at too high a level to involve individual schools fully. The situation was exacerbated by the fact that these 'joining up' structures were not yet fully bedded down in most places, and that the FSES initiative itself – aiming, as it did, to create one exceptional school in each local authority area – was hardly conducive to an authority-wide strategic approach. In practice, therefore, the majority of FSESs worked within local authority contexts that were supportive in practical terms, but that were not able to lock them into wider strategies and structures.

In many ways, this situation was replicated when they looked for strategic support to national policies and initiatives. Every Child Matters promised much, and began to be seen by school leaders as offering them a framework within which their own work could be located. However, in most areas, as we have seen, it was not as yet able to deliver working systems and resources. Similarly, at a time when central government was generating new initiatives, strategies and programmes at a rapid – some would say, alarming – rate, there was no shortage of places where schools could look for ideas, and, in some cases, funds. Typically, these initiatives offered schools (directly or through local authorities) additional funding in return for developing particular forms of provision, or pursuing particular targets. School leaders become skilled at 'bending' these initiatives and programmes to support their full service provision. For instance, schools could (like St James' College in the previous chapter) apply for 'specialist' status in one or other curriculum area – a status which required and resourced them to engage in community-oriented work and so could be used to support aspects of their full service provision. Others drew on the national initiatives for developing 'healthy schools' and reducing teenage pregnancies to develop health-related services, or associated themselves with a national crime prevention strategy as part of their work with vulnerable students, or secured purpose-built accommodation through a national schools rebuilding programme.

None of these initiatives and programmes, however, provided a comprehensive basis for an overall FSES strategy. As a result, school leaders often found themselves acting as 'bricoleurs', constructing as coherent an approach as they could out of these diverse opportunities and requirements. In one sense, this gave them considerable freedom of action, but it also meant that they were largely on their own, and that they were always likely to find coherence difficult to achieve. The ways in which they had to secure funding for their full service provision was central to this state of affairs – and it is to this that we turn next.

Funding and sustainability

In the English education system, the funding needed for staffing and other day-to-day running costs of schools is managed by the schools themselves. Local authorities retain relatively little money through which school budgets can be supplemented, though central government can do so through additional funding that is typically tied to projects and initiatives. Otherwise, when schools expand their activities, they have to find the funds themselves by looking to other sources.

As we saw in the previous chapter, FSESs received relatively generous seedcorn funding from government to support their provision. However, this was always time-limited and in any case did not cover the full costs of that provision. As a result, the process of bricolage could be seen at work again, as school leaders pursued multiple sources of funding. In the early stages, there were bitter complaints from many of them that this not only consumed large amounts of their time, but also made them answerable to multiple paymasters. They were concerned, in particular, that when the FSES project moneys dried up after three years, it would no longer be possible for them to sustain their provision.

In fact, these concerns seemed to ease as the project unfolded and as schools became more skilled in resourcing their work. The development of partnerships with other agencies was particularly important in this respect. Partly, this was because, in places where the 'joining up' of services was progressing well, pooled budgets began to become available which could be directed towards supporting some aspects of full service provision. Partly, it was because schools themselves worked hard at winning the trust of other agencies and showing how collaboration could bring mutual benefits. As a result, agencies became more willing to contribute their most valuable resource – their staff – to the school's provision. In at least two FSESs, for instance, the sustained provision of co-located social care professionals that was very precarious at the start of the initiative, had, three years later, been assured by the employing agencies. This was because they realized that locating their personnel in schools produced higher take-up rates, reduced no-shows at appointments, and enabled the agency to meet other key performance indicators. The situation was summed up neatly by the deputy head teacher of one FSES:

The physical capacity will be provided by the school, but if they are to be sustainable it is very much up to the other organizations, the partners involved in it. If they are not committed to locating their full service schools on a permanent basis to delivering from the schools, it won't happen, they won't be sustainable. That's the big leap that has to be made.

Given the problems of ensuring financial sustainability, schools tried to raise funds in whatever ways they could. Some of these were highly inventive. In one school a 'virtual FSES' had been set up using a telephone system that directed callers to workers from a range of agencies in the area. The school was piloting this system for the private company that had developed it. In return, they received a small fee for every call they fielded, and a small percentage of the purchase price of every new system that was sold – money which could be reinvested in the school's own extended provision. The same school operated a 'buy to let' system with a lorry it had purchased (the lorry was equipped with computing facilities and training rooms for community use). However, such entrepreneurship was unusual, and by far the commonest way of raising funds was to charge for participation in activities. This was a problematic issue for schools, though, who were ambivalent about whether they could or should lay charges on people who often had very low incomes. Some, therefore, decided to provide all their activities free.

Although for the most part schools became more confident of their ability to resource their provision as the initiative unfolded, this was not universal. Some dropped out altogether, and others thought that they could only sustain a scaled-down version of services and activities once direct government funding ceased at the end of the initiative. Many of them pointed to a tension, if not contradiction, between the importance of full service and extended schools in national policy, the seriousness with which schools and local authorities were setting about the development of provision and the limited and short-term nature of the funding stream available to support them. Put bluntly, many schools saw their full service provision as integral to their mission, yet the funding mechanisms to which they had access continued to treat it as a peripheral activity.

Accountability

At the time of the FSES initiative, schools in England were – and, indeed, continue to be – subject to a wide range of accountability mechanisms, most of them focusing intensively on the performance of the school's students in tests and examinations. Test results were publicly available and played a major part in shaping the reputation of the school, and so in determining how easy it is for the school to recruit students. There was also a national schools inspectorate – Ofsted – whose judgements on the quality of a school were also published, and could trigger interventions in its management. Local authorities kept a close eye on school performance and could, in certain circumstances, also intervene directly to change things. Schools had 'governing bodies' drawn from local stakeholders. They held the professionals in the school to account, but were themselves ultimately accountable for school performance. Finally, schools like those in the FSES initiative, which sought additional funding, were accountable through whatever mechanisms the providers of funding chose to use.

All of this created considerable ambiguities for FSESs. On the one hand, they were trying to develop provision which was aiming broadly at the well-being of students, their families and local communities. On the other hand, the most powerful forms of accountability were focused on 'standards' of student attainment. This ambiguity impacted most immediately on the way they conceptualized their FSES approach. As we saw in the previous chapter, there was a widespread assumption that a major purpose of extended provision was to overcome 'barriers to learning', and so to raise the standards of attainment for which schools were accountable. They might also want to generate other kinds of outcomes for other groups, but the accountability mechanisms in relation to such outcomes were less clearly defined, if they existed at all. Moreover, although they might see the outcomes of their full service provision emerging over relatively lengthy periods of time – school leaders often spoke in terms of a five to ten year time scale – attainment outcomes were assessed every year, and intervention in the school as a result of poor results could be swift.

The same ambiguity was evident in relation to Ofsted. In effect, Ofsted made judgements about school quality by assessing whether the school was operating in an approved manner and was producing outcomes – principally in terms of academic attainment – at adequate levels. This maintained the pressure on schools to drive up levels of attainment, particularly for FSESs which typically served low-attaining populations. At the same time, however, the basis on which Ofsted's judgements were made began to include elements that related more clearly to extended provision and to a wider range of outcomes. These changed expectations gave schools hope that their provision would be viewed favourably, and gave school leaders confidence that what they were doing was recognized in the accountability system. What was less certain, however, was how Ofsted would balance a favourable view of a school's extended provision against an unfavourable view of its students' attainments.

There was often uncertainty also about the nature of responsibilities for governing bodies. Governors were under the same pressure as head teachers to ensure that their schools produced the required levels of attainment outcomes. However, the growth of extended provision meant that they were taking on responsibility for areas of work that were outside their previous experience. Many of the issues were legal and financial in nature, such as the employment of non-teaching staff, commissioning of services, lettings policies, insurance, costings, and health and safety matters. It was, therefore, helpful that national guidance was published, and that many local authorities offered practical support. It was less helpful that these new responsibilities added to what was already the considerable difficulty of finding governors in disadvantaged areas with the skills and confidence to take on the challenge of running schools (Dean et al., 2007).

A final issue in relation to accountability was that schools had no easy way of demonstrating that their full service provision was having any significant effects. In England, systems for monitoring attainment outcomes are relatively sophisticated and can be accessed and used easily by schools. There are measures of other kinds of outcomes – in relation, for instance to health and crime – at area level, but they are held by other agencies. At the time of the FSES initiative, schools did not routinely have (and arguably had not hitherto needed) access to such data, and systems were only now beginning to develop which might give them this access. FSESs also lacked an appropriate methodology for evaluating the impact of their provision. Drawing on their experience with attainment data, they saw evaluation in terms of simple input-output models. Many of them thought, therefore, that they should be collecting base-line data so that they could see the effects of their provision when they collected the equivalent data some time later. Unfortunately, they immediately hit snags. As one local authority manager explained: 'lots of the measures that Government wants are on targets where there isn't any baseline data'.

They also found that, whilst this model might work with children whose attainments were routinely tested, it was much more problematic in the case of services and activities being offered to voluntary participants. As one FSES manager acknowledged:

> To measure it you need to have a baseline. But if the first thing you do when somebody walks through the door is . . . 'what do you think about yourself and how many "O" levels [examination passes] have you got?', then actually you frighten them off, you're not going to keep them . . . That is the biggest issue in my head. How we get the baseline, without frightening people off.

Moreover, even where schools were able to collect data – and most of them kept registers of attendance or asked participants in activities to fill in satisfaction sheets – they were baffled as to how they might use those data to show the impacts of their provision. It is for this reason, amongst others, that we spend time in the next chapter explaining our own evaluation methodology and how it might be adapted by full service and extended schools.

Consultation or participation?

Offering additional services and activities took FSESs into uncharted territory, in the sense that it shifted their work from an obligatory to a voluntary basis. In their standard teaching role, they were dealing with children who were (in principle at least) obliged to attend and to accept whatever the school set before them. However, in their extended roles, schools were offering activities that had to be attractive enough to entice participants to take them up, or services that users felt met their needs. They were, moreover, ostensibly working in the best interests of children, families and local people rather than simply acting as part of a state-controlled education system. This raised the question of how they should engage with and respond to the people on whose behalf they were supposedly acting.

All of the FSESs we worked with saw themselves as being in the business of 'consulting' students, parents and community members. This took a variety of forms: audits of existing provision; consulting student representatives on the school council; using parenting support sessions to listen to people's concerns; setting up parent groups; giving parents the opportunity to socialize and share concerns; setting up 'parent consultation days' to discuss children's progress as opposed to traditional parents' evenings; administering questionnaires to pupils and parents; commissioning private consultations; and going out onto the street with clip-boards to consult with the community. Where possible, schools drew on existing data that had already been collected by another agency or initiative working in the area. A key facilitating factor in developing these strategies was the involvement of staff – whether employed by the school or by partner agencies – who were not themselves teachers. They were in a position to engage in more thorough consultations than teachers could have managed, and were often able to develop less guarded relationships with children and adults whose trust needed to be won before they would provide useful information. In this respect, family support workers or non-teacher extended school coordinators often proved to be very useful assets.

Despite this, many FSESs reported considerable challenges in this area. Participation in consultation was often low, and school staff felt that much of what people said they wanted to happen was impracticable. For their part, those who were consulted were sometimes skeptical about how far yet another consultation would make any difference to their lives, and in any case tended to be divided about what they wanted. Underlying these difficulties were some deep ambiguities about what consultation meant, and, beyond this, about how an FSES should relate to children, families and communities. In some cases, school personnel were simply frustrated by the reluctance of people to engage with them. The reason, we were told on more than one occasion, was that such people were 'hard to reach' and that efforts to do so were almost invariably futile. In other cases, schools recognized that consultation was difficult, but felt that it was worth persevering with so that the school could offer something more attractive to local people. As one FSES coordinator explained: 'You can't underestimate consultation actually with the community. You can think of something that you think is going to work really well and then it doesn't . . . You can't make assumptions about what they want out there'.

It was a small step from this to recognizing that school personnel actually knew very little about the lives of the people they were hoping to benefit. 'This has got to come from the community', one head teacher told us:

> It can't come from us, sitting in schools, saying, 'Actually we think this poor deprived community needs a little bit of this and a little bit of that'. What on earth do we know? . . . It won't work and they wouldn't come otherwise.

All of these approaches viewed consultation as a means of finding out 'what people want' and then providing it. However, there were some places where different models began to emerge. Some FSES leaders realized that the barriers to local people's engagement with the school were not simply that the school was offering the wrong kinds of services and activities, but that there was something about the very fact that it was a school that deterred engagement. In some ways, it was the wrong kind of institution. One, for instance, spoke of the 'contradiction' between the school's efforts to work with local people, and the fences, cameras and other 'symbolic barriers' it erected between itself and them. Where school leaders saw that this was a problem, they tried various strategies to overcome it. Some thought that the best way was to engage in what they saw as the 'risky' business of holding consultation events where straight talking was encouraged. Others tried to involve local people directly in the strategic management of extended provision. Beyond this, a few schools saw themselves as on a journey from providing for the needs of children and local people, or responding to their requests, to handing over control of their extended provision to them. As one head argued:

> it had to be, because of the nature of the community here, owned by the community and it's going to have to be led by the community eventually. Needs are going to have to be identified and resources are going to have to be evaluated by the people who use them.

Another put the issue rather succinctly: 'Who are the key people that actively need to drive this? I think it is young people themselves. I passionately believe that . . . I think we sometimes have the horse and the cart in the wrong order'.

Some conclusions

To some extent, it is possible to see the issues we have just described as no more than teething problems, arising as schools began to adopt new ways of working, and as local and national policy makers began to develop new frameworks within which these new practices could flourish. There is plenty of evidence for this. It is certainly the case that many of the problems reported by schools in the early days of the FSES initiative were likely to have been resolved by the end of the initiative some three years later. It is also true that the major national policy frameworks – notably, the development of integrated services under the aegis of Every Child Matters – were being put in place at the same time as the FSES initiative was running. They were by no means fully bedded down, and did not therefore provide schools with the kinds of certainty and support that they might reasonably have hoped for in the course of time. Moreover, the FSES initiative itself was just that – a time-limited initiative, encouraging local experimentation rather than implementing a tried and tested model.

On the other hand, treating these issues simply as teething problems may underestimate their implications. What is striking about them, it seems to us, is that they arise from a transition process between different models of what schools are and should be. Whatever new forms of provision they might be developing, all of the schools in the initiative were, first and foremost, schools like any others. As such, they had a clearly defined role – to educate children – and the personnel, management structures, funding and established sets of practices to carry out that role. If they needed support and guidance, they could turn to their local authorities and a range of other agencies. If they wanted to know how they were doing, they could draw on the rich array of performance data to which they had access. And when, as happened on a regular basis, they were called to account, at least it was against criteria that were transparent, however much the schools themselves might sometimes regard them as unfair.

However, as these schools began to develop full service provision, such certainties disappeared. As we have seen, established management and staffing structures came to seem inadequate. Funding, which was relatively stable for their 'core business', became uncertain. Support was available, but on key issues of what they were supposed to be achieving and how, it was much less clear than they had been used to. Accountability mechanisms, meanwhile, came to seem inappropriate and therefore even more unfair than was previously the case. In other words, the schools were moving into uncharted waters, or, to put it another way, they were crossing the boundaries between their established practices and new possibilities for action.

The concepts of 'boundary work' (Edwards *et al.*, 2009, 2010) and 'boundary crossing' (Kerosuo and Engestrom, 2003; Tsui and Law, 2007; Tuomi-Grohn and Engestrom, 2007) have begun to be used extensively to explain what happens when organizations (and, therefore, their personnel) encounter new situations, new problems and new ways of working – and specifically what is happening in schools in England as they embrace the wider Every Child Matters agenda. Such situations create the possibility of organizational learning, but, as Edwards *et al.* (2010) point out, they also create the possibility that organizations will simply reinforce their existing boundaries. To some extent, the issues we have outlined here can be explained in this way. It seems clear that FSESs, to differing extents, viewed the uncertainties of their new role as an opportunity to learn. They found new management structures, employed new kinds of staff, developed new relationships with other agencies, and used resources in a new way. There were even small signs that some schools were starting to take account of the complex politics of extended schools. As we have seen, a few began to think deeply about their stance towards the children, families and communities they served, breaking out of their traditional knowledge-transmission role, and beginning to see themselves as enablers and facilitators for people who were capable of taking control of their own lives (Todd, 2007).

At the same time, it is also clear that there were strong incentives for schools, if not exactly to reinforce their existing boundaries, then at least to manage their new role in ways which did not threaten them too much. This could be seen in those cases where extended provision functioned as an add-on to an otherwise unchanged set of school practices, where its management and staffing remained separate from the rest of the school, or where activities and services were seen as entirely dependent on a separate funding stream. It could also be seen in schools' continued prioritization of student attainment, and in the deficit-oriented and somewhat paternalistic views of local people which surfaced from time to time.

Our assessment is that there were not two distinct types of schools in the FSES initiative, but that all schools experienced these tensions to some extent. Indeed, the ambiguities and uncertainties we noted in the Beresford, Clark and St James' schools (in the previous chapter) can perhaps best be explained as resulting from tensions of this kind. This is, we suggest, partly because the pull of established practices and cultures must be strong in any attempt at boundary crossing, but also partly because all the schools were working within the same national policy context. The ambiguity and, in respect of the development of FSESs, the inadequacy of that context is inescapable. Certainly, it had positive elements – the encouragement for schools to develop extended provision, the additional funding, the practical support, and the nascent local networks of 'joined up' services and decision-making. However, it also had many elements which encouraged schools to remain within their existing boundaries – the failure to lock schools into local strategies, the uncertainty over funding, and, above all, the continued emphasis on a narrowly constructed standards agenda and the high-stakes accountability mechanisms that enforced that agenda. Not surprisingly, therefore, the boundary zone for FSESs was a deeply ambiguous and, in some ways, dangerous one.

We draw two conclusions from this. One is that the transition from 'school' to 'full service and extended school' is a challenging one for those who try to make the change. It demands a willingness to learn, to take risks, and to question fundamental assumptions. It means rethinking how the school is managed, funded and staffed, how it relates its established purposes and practices to its new ones, and how it relates to the children and adults it seeks to serve. The second is that the extent to which schools are successful in this transition is likely to depend to a significant degree on the support they receive from national and local policy frameworks. Policy needs to offer schools sustainable resourcing and staffing for their new roles, and to locate them within a functioning system of public services, particularly in areas of disadvantage. It needs to ensure that school leaders understand those roles and have the knowledge and skills to lead schools through the transition process. It needs to ensure that schools are held to account for the outcomes that full service and extended provision is intended to generate, and not for some other or more limited set of outcomes. It needs to offer some clarity not just about what they are intended to do, but about why they are intended to do it. Ultimately, in other words, it needs to offer schools a vision of what they are and what they are for, and to equip them with the tools they need to turn that vision into a reality. Perhaps above all, it needs to encourage the kind of reflective criticality in schools that we believed we could begin to see emerging in some places.

With this in mind, it might be worth bearing in mind some of the more positive aspects of education policy in England that were being put in place during the lifetime of the FSES initiative, and to which we have referred in earlier chapters. We are thinking here of the development of integrated children's services; of the articulation of a common set of aims for those services; of the realignment of schools as part of those services; of the local and national structures for formulating 'joined up' strategies; and of the policy commitments to end child poverty and tackle social exclusion. We also have in mind the shift during the lifetime of the FSES initiative from the idea of a few, exceptional, full service and extended schools to the expectation that every school would offer access to extended services, and that it would therefore become part of a network of provision based on progressive universalist principles. The point is not that policy makers in England had got things right – far from it – but that their sometimes hesitant and ambiguous efforts in this period demonstrate what *might* be possible. This is a theme to which we shall return in later chapters.

Chapter 5

Issues in evaluation

In previous chapters, we have seen how high hopes have been attached to full service and extended schools. Rethinking the role of schools and reconfiguring services around schools, advocates have claimed, will overcome educational disadvantage, or preserve threatened communities, or, even, build a new kind of society. Such claims are doubtless energising, but they mean little if they cannot be substantiated. Unless we know what outcomes full service and extended schools are capable of generating, and how best to secure those outcomes, there is a real danger that substantial effort and resource will be expended on developments which make little real difference to children, families and communities. Moreover, we saw in the last chapter how partial and inappropriate mechanisms for holding English schools to account have undermined their development of extended provision. Unless, therefore, the performance of schools is judged in ways that are sensitive to the aims and outcomes of full service and extended approaches, we should expect the development of such approaches to be unnecessarily problematic.

These issues were particularly important for our work on the Full Service Extended Schools (FSES) initiative in England. We were commissioned by the government to evaluate not only what schools were doing, the difficulties they faced and the solutions they were discovering, but also to find evidence as to whether they were making any difference to the lives of the children and adults with whom they worked. At a time when the 'standards agenda' dominated much thinking about what schools were and were for, this inevitably meant identifying impacts on children's attainments. However, it also meant doing so in a way which did justice to the wider aims of the FSES initiative itself, and of full service and extended school approaches in general.

The problems of evaluation

Internationally, the evaluation of full service and extended schools has proved to be anything but straightforward. Despite a substantial literature in the field, there is, as Wilkin *et al.* point out, 'little systematic, rigorous evaluation of the concept and its implementation' (2003b, p. 5). There appear to be a number of reasons for this. One is the preponderance in the literature of how-to-do-it guides and advocacy texts. Another is what seems to be a sense that full service approaches are so self-evidently the right thing to do that searching for robust evidence is almost unnecessary. As one US-based review comments:

> It seems intuitively obvious that creating a context that interweaves home, school, and community, and that makes students valued and contributing members should have a powerful effect on student learning. But attempts to connect community collaborations and student test scores have been few and contradictory.
>
> (Keyes and Gregg, 2001, p. 40)

However, even where outcomes evaluations have been attempted, they have tended to succumb either to their own limitations or to the inherent complexity of the task, or both. Attainment outcomes, for instance, may be difficult to identify. There may be important individual gains which become invisible when aggregated at the school level. Alternatively, other schools may be adopting different strategies for raising attainment, so that the gains from full service and extended approaches are hidden. Even when changes in levels of attainment can be found, as Blank *et al.* (2003, pp. 46–47) report, they frequently run up against the problem of attribution. Full service and extended approaches are typically complex and varied, encompassing very different areas of intervention (youth development, education, parent involvement, community building, and so on). It is difficult to say, therefore, which aspect of the school's approach has produced what outcomes. Indeed, it may be something quite different from the school's full service provision that is having the effect. An evaluation of a Chicago full service schools initiative (FSSI), for instance, found some evidence of improved student attainment outcomes, but could not reliably attribute this to the development of full service provision: 'Many efforts were underway in each school during the FSSI period to improve student outcomes, and no simple causal links can be drawn between FSSI and improvement at the three schools' (Whalen, 2002, p. 2).

We might add that, since many full service and extended school initiatives focus on schools in highly disadvantaged areas, those schools are particularly likely to be using all sorts of other strategies to drive up children's achievements. Indeed, in some cases – 'Comer' schools being an obvious case in point (Comer and Emmons, 2006) – elements of full service and extended school approaches are consciously combined with wider school improvement approaches, making the attribution of effects to one or other element very difficult. Despite the claims in the advocacy literature, therefore, the reality, as Henderson and Mapp argue, is that: 'Many conclusions have to be carefully hedged because little can be said about cause and effect' (Henderson and Mapp, 2002, p. 18). To complicate matters further, of course, whilst most full service and extended schools see attainment outcomes as important, these are unlikely to be the only ones at which they aim. They may, as we have seen, be trying to enhance the support families can offer their children, or equip local people with the skills they need to survive in the labour market, or improve people's sense of well-being, or change community cultures. Outcomes of this kind are difficult to evaluate, not least because there are often no usable outcome measures, and because it may simply not be possible to wait until the full effects of full service provision are felt. As the evaluators of the Children's Aid Society Community Schools in New York argue: 'community schools are complex systems making fundamental institutional changes, and this means that events occur in many ways and on many levels'. It is therefore 'necessary to look beyond standardized test scores to understand the impact of community schools' (Clark and Grimaldi, 2005, p. 173).

In the circumstances, what is needed, it would appear, are sophisticated evaluation designs, using a range of ways of identifying outcomes. If we then add that, even if outcomes can be identified, they may only materialize after some years, it is clear that evaluations need also to be long term. Yet the reality is that many evaluations are under-resourced, and therefore under-powered. School leaders and sponsors of initiatives usually want to know whether their work is having any effect – but they understandably want to know quickly and without diverting too much funding from provision into evaluators' bank accounts. As Henderson and Mapp's review of the research evidence concludes:

> There is . . . not enough long-term research because of the limits of funding for such ambitious work. Many studies have small samples, while others depend on self-reports rather than independent verification.
>
> (Henderson and Mapp, 2002, p. 18)

We faced all of these problems when we began our evaluation of the FSES initiative in England, but there were also further complicating factors. That initiative was, as we have seen, simply the latest in a long line of full service and extended school developments in our country. Not surprisingly, therefore, some FSESs had already developed substantial extended provision well before the initiative got under way, as had many other schools outside the initiative. This made the idea of basing the evaluation on comparison – either of participating and non-participating schools, or of participating schools before and after joining the initiative – highly problematic. Moreover, as we saw in chapter three, at the start of the national initiative, participating schools were given a list of areas in which they were expected to develop activities (DfES, 2003b, 2003c), and were given some additional funding to support this development. Beyond this, there was more or less unlimited flexibility for individual schools to determine what provision they would develop and how. There was, therefore, at least as much variation between FSESs as there was between them and other schools.

We encountered one of the consequences of this open specification as soon as we began our preliminary fieldwork with schools. It became clear that not only were schools setting up different forms of provision within the broad areas specified by national guidance, but that the boundaries around the FSES initiative in each school, and between it and other initiatives, were far from clear. When we asked school leaders to describe their provision, they typically listed a whole range of services and activities, some of which they had developed in response to the FSES initiative, but many of which were established and funded in response to other national initiatives, or were part of school-led developments, or were long-established aspects of provision in the school. Moreover, they did this in different ways. Two of the schools, for instance, had on-site 'Community Learning Centres', developed as part of a separate initiative. These centres gave community members and school students access to computing facilities and could act as the base for adult learning provision. One of the schools saw the centre as an integral part of its FSES approach, giving it a way of impacting on engagement with learning amongst the local adult population and increasing the skill levels in that population. Another saw it as nothing to do with its approach. School leaders were quite happy that the centre should be engaging with local communities, but their ambitions for the school's full service provision did not include this kind of engagement.

It became clear that school leaders were seeing the FSES initiative simply as a skeleton of requirements and funding, which they needed to flesh out by putting together different combinations of resources, services and activities, in pursuit of more or less explicitly articulated aims. This distinctive combination of ends and means we began to refer to as the school's 'approach' – a term we have continued to use in this book. The notion of an approach is important for understanding what it was that we needed to evaluate. This was neither a tightly bounded national initiative, nor a clearly defined 'model' of full service provision, nor again – in most cases, at least – simply a set of activities loosely bundled together. As the accounts of schools we outlined in chapter three illustrate, what we were presented with were more or less coherent (albeit often not explicitly articulated) attempts to marshal a wide range of actions in order to generate an almost equally wide range of outcomes that school leaders felt to be valuable.

Designing the evaluation

Taking all of these factors into account, it did not seem to us possible to rely on a simple input-output evaluation design. We could not credibly treat the FSES initiative as an intervention that was the same in every school, deploy a limited range of outcome measures in those schools, and compare the results with outcomes where the intervention was not in place. Our response, therefore, was twofold. First, we opted for a multi-strand, mixed methods design, in the expectation that different strands would illuminate different aspects of a complex phenomenon. Second, we placed at the core of that design the approach to evaluation to which we have referred earlier in this book – theory of change methodology. The technical details of each of these strands are described in more detail in our evaluation reports (Cummings et al., 2005, 2006, 2007a). Later on, we give a brief account of each before exploring how we used the theory of change methodology in a sample of case study schools, and what its implications are for the development of full service and extended schools.

Statistical analysis of the National Pupil Database

The English school system is particularly rich in statistical data relating to the attainments of school students. The National Pupil Database (NPD) holds data at

individual pupil level on attainments in national tests, teacher assessments and examinations. It also records a range of other information about each student, including
school attended, gender, entitlement to free school meals (a broad indicator of low
family income), ethnicity and special educational needs status. Analyses of NPD are
used widely by researchers and government statisticians in England to compare the
attainments of different groups of students, the effects of attendance at different
types of schools, and the impacts of particular projects and initiatives. Because the
database holds so much information about students, statisticians are able to identify a
variable in which they are interested (ethnicity, say, or family income) and show what
effect it has when all the other variables are controlled for.

We were able to use NPD in just this way. By identifying in the database which
schools were and were not FSESs, we could use attendance at an FSES as a variable,
exploring its effect on attainment. In particular, we were able to search not only for
an overall 'FSES effect', but also for differential effects on different groups of students – for instance, those entitled to free school meals or identified as having special
educational needs. Doing so, of course, does not overcome the evaluation problems
we outlined earlier in relation to focusing overly on attainment and looking for clear
differences between FSESs and other 'types' of schools. Our view, therefore, was
that the evaluation as a whole could not be built solely on this strand, though it might
make a contribution to the overall picture.

Cost benefit analysis

Although a concern with attainment outcomes – and, indeed, other kinds of outcomes
for children, families and communities – is important, it is only one way of assessing the kinds of impacts an initiative might have. Cost benefit analysis (CBA) works,
quite literally, with a different evaluation currency – the currency of monetary values.
It takes the kinds of outcomes with which we are familiar – raised educational attainments, for instance, or improved health – and recognizes that they have a monetary
value, not just to the individual, but to the economy as a whole. So, for instance, getting young people to attend school, desist from criminal activities, take fewer health
risks and attain more highly has all sorts of benefits for the young people themselves.
However, it also means that they are more likely to become productive contributors
to the economy, whilst fewer resources are consumed by, say, policing their behaviour, or providing them with health care. At the same time, producing 'benefits' of
this kind also incurs 'costs', because resources have to be invested in order to generate positive outcomes. This is true whether or not money changes hands at the point
where resources are put to use.

Cost benefit analysis involves identifying all the costs and benefits in an activity
and using a set of standard procedures to determine their monetary value. Whilst on
the face of it this appears to be a somewhat reductionist approach, in fact it gives us
a very different way of asking about 'value' and 'value for money' from that which
most educational evaluations deploy. In particular, it offers a way of quantifying and
comparing outcomes that might otherwise be dismissed as being unimportant. For

instance, full service and extended schools often seek to have the kinds of impacts on young people's engagement with learning, anti-social behaviour and health that we alluded to earlier. Cost benefit analysis foregrounds those impacts and allocates a monetary value to them which often turns out to be surprisingly high. In so doing, it helps us guard against the assumption that the impacts of what schools do can only reliably be measured in terms of improvements in attainment.

In the evaluation of the FSES initiative, we carried out a cost benefit analysis in 10 schools. This involved an iterative process of discussion with school leaders, aimed at identifying the outcomes their full service provision was producing and the inputs (funding, staff time, volunteer time and so on) they were using to sustain their provision. Given the difficulties of quantifying both outcomes and inputs, a good deal of estimation was necessary, but on the basis of these estimates monetary values were derived for costs and benefits.

Other methods

The analysis of NPD aside, much of the evaluation depended on detailed interaction with small numbers of schools, and relied heavily on what individuals within those schools told us. It was important, therefore, that we were able to set our findings in a wider context. We did this in three ways:

1. We sent a questionnaire to all FSESs in the initiative, asking them, amongst other things, about resourcing and funding, services and activities, and outcomes.
2. We undertook a series of field visits to nine 'comparator' schools, chosen to be similar to schools in our theory of change case study sample, but to be working outside the FSES initiative. The field visits tried to identify how far schools outside the initiative were offering similar kinds of provision, and how they addressed the problems and needs to which FSESs saw their full service provision as a response.
3. We administered some brief questionnaires to staff and a sample of students and parents in our case study schools and the comparator schools, to explore how positively respondents in the different schools felt about themselves and about the levels of support offered by the schools.

The theory of change strand

Although each of these methods contributed to the overall evaluation, the core of our work centred on eliciting and testing the theories of change underpinning the work of a sample of FSESs. Theory of change is one of a family of theory-based approaches to evaluation (Stame, 2004; Weiss, 1995) that start from the assumption that purposeful activity implies a 'theory of action' (Argyris and Schön, 1978, 1996). In other words, people taking action do so on the assumption that, in a given context, those actions will bring about a set of changes that will ultimately lead to some intended outcomes. As an evaluation strategy, the theory of change approach involves 'a systematic and cumulative study of the links between activities, outcomes and context of the initiative' (Connell and Kubisch, 1998, p. 16). Typically, therefore, evaluators work with actors to surface how they understand the situation in which they find themselves, what outcomes they intend to generate, and how they believe their actions will lead to these outcomes.

Theories of change are effectively predictions of what is going to happen as a result of particular actions. Once the theory is articulated, it becomes possible to ask how coherent it is, how likely it is that the intended outcomes will materialize, and what needs to be put in place so that the reality unfolds as predicted by the theory. It also becomes possible to ask what evidence might indicate that such a process was in train – in other words, that the intermediate changes predicted by the theory were beginning to happen, and that outcomes either were materializing already, or were likely to do so in the future.

From our point of view, an evaluation of this kind had many advantages. First, it made no assumptions about what sorts of action FSESs should be taking, or what kinds of outcomes they might aim at. It recognized that schools would have different 'approaches', and that the only way to find out what these were was to engage with the detail of what each school was doing and what the leaders of each school presented as their aims. Second, by tracking intermediate changes, it had a means of linking end-point outcomes to actions. While this did not entirely remove the problem of attribution (because other actions that were not being tracked might also be playing a part), it did at least make it possible to demonstrate the likelihood that some specific action or set of actions had set in train a series of changes, and that those changes had in turn led to one or more outcomes. Moreover, if the outcomes had not materialized by the end of the evaluation period, it would still be possible to show whether changes were happening in such a way as to make those outcomes more or less likely. Finally, it gave the school leaders with whom we were working something in return for their willingness to take part in the evaluation. It helped them think through what they were trying to achieve, gave them feedback on the coherence of their plans, and gave them early indications of whether things were moving in the direction they intended. Since school leaders in England have grown accustomed to being set targets externally for the outcomes they are expected to 'deliver', and are then likely to be subject to a punitive response if they fail to produce these outcomes, they typically found this more collaborative and supportive response a welcome change.

There is no established toolkit for theory of change evaluations (Mackenzie and Blamey, 2005); it is itself an 'approach' (Connell and Kubisch, 1998) rather than a highly specified evaluation method. Using it in the evaluation of FSESs, therefore, was a matter of taking its broad principles and adapting them to the particular context in which we were working. Again, a full technical account of how we undertook the evaluation is provided in our project reports. In essence, however, we identified 17 schools with which to work in depth. This sample reflected the range of school types and contexts in the initiative as a whole. So, we included primary, secondary, and special schools, schools in different local authority areas, schools whose populations had different ethnic compositions, and schools in inner cities, suburbs and small towns. We knew about these schools from the large amount of data that are available publicly on English schools, and from some brief 'mapping' visits we had undertaken with a larger sample. The schools in the sample were diverse, but, like most schools in the initiative, were serving disadvantaged areas. In addition, we deliberately selected schools where full service provision was relatively well developed, so that there was a realistic chance of being able to identify its impacts and outcomes. This last point is significant, particularly given that most schools in the initiative were volunteers, and that only those with a high level of commitment were likely to agree to have their work evaluated. It meant in effect that we were not evaluating the overall outcomes of the national initiative so much as the outcomes of full service and extended approaches in particular schools where conditions were broadly favourable. We were therefore concerned with what these approaches *could* achieve in the right circumstances, rather than with what they *did* achieve in every case.

The fieldwork in schools involved three broad stages, aimed at working with schools to surface and articulate the theories of change underpinning the services and activities they were providing:

- *Stage 1*: Development and clarification of an outline theory of change, specifying: the situation which the school leaders saw themselves as facing (that is, the challenges faced by the school and the needs and resources of students, families and communities locally); the main strands of actions being taken (i.e. a more generalized conceptualization of what was often a diverse range of services and activities in terms of a smaller number of more or less discrete areas of operation); and the long-term outcomes envisaged as a result of the strands of action (i.e. the ways in which the school anticipated that this situation would be changed by FSES provision).
- *Stage 2*: Development of a chart of intermediate changes that the FSES expected would occur as a result of these actions, in order to bring about the anticipated outcomes.
- *Stage 3*: Development of an evaluation plan to show the evidence that the schools and the evaluation team would collect in order to determine whether the intermediate changes were occurring as predicted.

Working through these stages meant spending a good deal of time with school leaders, discussing with them what provision they were trying to develop and why. Articulating theories of change, however, was not an easy process. The accounts given by interviewees were usually not structured in a way that was easily compatible with our needs as evaluators. Broadly speaking, they provided us with a large amount of descriptive detail rather than a coherent analysis of the links between situation, actions and outcomes. They were very happy to list the problems in the area (as they saw them) and the multiple actions that the school was taking. However, they found it more difficult to organize those 'problems' in some hierarchical way that differentiated between underlying causes and surface effects, or to organize their actions into coherent strands, or to be precise about the outcomes they expected to result from their work. They found the request to identify a sequence of intermediate changes particularly challenging. This was partly because the process whereby an action produced an outcome seemed to them self-evident and in no need of explication. Partly, it was because they found it hard to disentangle how things would change for their intended beneficiaries (the 'outcomes') from the way in which they as professionals would do things differently (the 'outputs'). In other words, we were working with school leaders whose work was all about using their professional judgement to identify what needed to be done and then making sure that it got done. Until we began to press them, they had neither the opportunity nor need to spend time making explicit what they believed about the situations they faced and the impacts their actions might have.

In this situation, we found that a partnership approach worked well, in which evaluators and school leaders pooled their different kinds of knowledge and skill. Using what the school leaders told us in interviews, we took responsibility for progressively clarifying and modelling for and with them an account of their theory of change. For each stage we produced diagrams and text which they could amend or reject as they saw fit. Although some theory of change methodologists advocate that theories should be articulated 'in fine detail' (Weiss, 1995), our experience was just the opposite. Since the school leaders we were working with were already immersed in the detail of what they were doing, our task was to abstract from what they said the broad structures of their underlying theories. We therefore began with a 'mapping grid' (see Figure 5.1 for an example from 'Keith' High School). See also Dyson and Todd (2010) where Figure 5.1 first appeared. This recorded what school leaders told us in a first round of interviews, but organized it in a particular way. What were often wide-ranging discussions were set out in terms of a loosely structured theory of change – that is, in terms of the situation school leaders saw the school as facing, the actions they were taking, and the intermediate and long-term outcomes they expected to produce, with a note about structures in the school and any relevant contextual factors. This enabled our partners in schools – sometimes, they told us, for the first time – to see what they were doing as a structured intervention rather than as a somewhat hectic round of loosely connected activities. Once this was agreed as an accurate representation of what the school was trying to do, we developed an even more simplified diagram (see Figure 5.2) which tried to remove all complexity in order to reveal the underlying structure of the school's theory of change.

This simplified diagram confronted school leaders with the basic assumptions that underpinned what they were doing. Typically, it had to be negotiated and renegotiated a number of times until they were satisfied that those assumptions were captured accurately, and that they were ones with which they could be comfortable. It was then possible to reintroduce a degree of complexity by working with them on the question of how actions were expected to be linked to outcomes through a series of intermediate changes. We found it helped school leaders to focus on intended beneficiaries rather than on their own plans if we asked them to think about what might happen to a particular individual who accessed a service or took part in an activity. How, we

Situation analysis

The school is situated in a deprived area that has seen the decline of local industry. The community is characterized by:

- High unemployment
- Low aspiration
- Insular, inward looking community
- Poor housing, poor health
- Teenage pregnancy highest in city
- High social exclusion
- Domestic violence, debt
- Drug related crime, prostitution
- Over 90% of adult workers are women. Young men don't identify with the kind of work where opportunities arise

School analysis

- School amalgamated several times
- Catchment is covered by 2 Sure Start projects
- Unused rooms ripe for refurbishment and community development
- 5 years ago it was a sink school
- A-Cs were 6%. By 2003, up to 30%
- FSM 55% take-up, but entitlement of 70%
- Need for YPs access to health, new approach to get them onsite
- School aggression
- Low attainment
- Low achievement
- Low aspiration

There is a (i) lack of social capacity, (ii) compounded by deprivation, (iii) which has an impact on achievement at school level.

Actions, activities & provision

- Multi-agency centre used by health, social services and youth service (PFI ownership)
- Clinic-in-a-box
- Fast tracking kids on the curriculum
- Parents as classroom assistants
- FSES co-ordinator (school parent)
- Crèche facilities
- School newsletter; school CD
- Adult education. GNVQ classes
- Staff job description includes community working
- Youth club facility (planned)
- Development of the disused garages into centre for pre-school groups, WorkStart and other agencies. Works alongside the growth of the Community Learning Centre and library
- Increase car parking capacity (planned)
- LearnDirect onsite
- Links with local college, & universities
- Links with parents+ community through the local residents association
- Feeder primary will become site for Sure Start centre and 1st Children's Centre
- Targeting groups e.g. adult project ownersh p
- Summer school (Yr 11)

Structures

Management
- Created a multi-agency steering group, behaviour attendance group
- Moved the chair of the group away from the LEA so that it is perceived as genuine multi-agency and not an education LEA led forum

Infrastructure
- Redevelopment of the garages into multi agency centre

Funding
- Sure Start
- BIP
- EiC
- Bid for 'community green spaces' programme (help improve sports facilities)

Sustainability
- Juggling in terms of resource procurement
- Income generation
- FSES embedded into school philosophy

Intermediate outcomes

- Former pupils employed as modern apprentices and professionals from other local agencies now based on school site
- Re-engage parents and wider community with the school
- Re-engage parents back into employment
- Revitalizing the school
- Shared adult and young person learning
- Adults taking ownership of an initiative

Relevant contextual factors – policies & initiatives

- The school was nominated by the EiC partnership on the strength of its existing extended work and the most challenging social indicators
- From a partnership point of view, LA has 9 strands of EiC, the extended school is very much part of the BIP strand
- FSES criteria: socio-economic data, school history, plans for behaviour support

Long-term outcomes

- Raised aspiration of school and community
- A multi-agency, co-ordinated approach to community developments
- Potential for regeneration through learning within the community
- Drive to raise standards
- Meeting the needs of young people so that the school is actually impacting on home, family and community as well as academically
- Raise attainment
- Raise school profile
- Raise achievement
- Ownership of the future
- Healthier, wealthier community will meet its own needs by creating its own solutions
- Community determining their own outcome

Figure 5.1 A school's mapping grid.

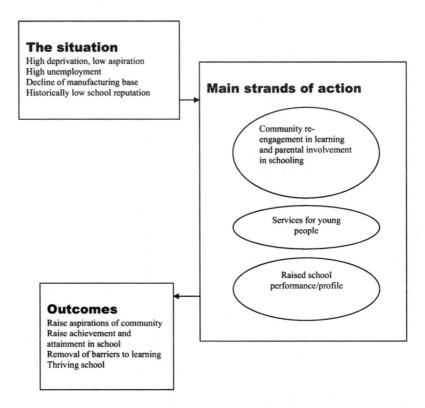

Figure 5.2 Simplified diagram of a school's theory of change.

asked them, would this change things for this person in the first instance? What would then happen to them? What would change next for them – and so on until a chain of impacts was built up leading to some intended outcome.

Once we had mapped all of this out, the theory of change was fully articulated and we were able to move onto the third stage – the development of an evaluation plan. We discussed with school leaders the sort of evidence which might demonstrate that any change in the sequence was indeed taking place. Where possible, we identified evidence that the school already had to hand or was proposing to collect, supplementing this with data that we ourselves could collect. This evidence might well include familiar outcomes indicators, such as measures of student attainment. However, it was by no means restricted to these, since anything which indicated whether changes were or were not happening as predicted was of use. We therefore could include whatever kinds of data were relevant to this purpose, including surveys of activity participants, anecdotes from service providers, registers of attendance at activities, and interviews with professionals, service users and activity participants. The final product of the work to articulate the theory of change, therefore, was an evaluation plan setting out the main strands of action, the sequence of changes expected to result from those actions, and the sorts of evidence which might demonstrate these changes. An extract from one such plan is presented as Figure 5.3.

With this plan in place, we were then able to set about collecting the evidence it specified. Again, this was an iterative process in which school leaders were closely

LEA: Townville	SCHOOL: Keith High	
Strands of action	Intermediate changes	What data shows this is happening?
STRAND 1: Community re-engagement in learning and parental involvement in schooling	The general community re-engage with the school through community links	Data on: • Participation rates Interviews with: • Community groups
	Hard to reach adults receive targeted support (e.g. via the Probation Service)	Data on: • Referrals Interviews with: • Probation service • Adults on probation
	Barriers to learning are removed (practical e.g. minibus support, and personal)	Interviews with: • Adults (e.g. on probation)
	Aspirations raised (STEPS programme for parents, MATRIX award, Investors in Excellence for YP, parents, community members, professionals)	Data on: • Participation rates • Agency targets Interviews with: • Parents • Community groups • Young persons • Agency professionals
	Some parents begin to work in school (e.g. employment as Teaching Assistants or voluntary work)	Data on: • Recruitment records Interviews with: • Parents (as Teaching Assistants) • Parents involved in other school capacity
	Some adults helped back into the workplace by accessing qualifications on the school site ('Destinations' & WEA, Next Steps)	Data on: • Employment records Interviews with: • Employers
	Community thinks positively about the school as an environment for lifelong learning	Interviews with: • School staff • Parents • Community groups • Pupils • Families

Figure 5.3 Extract from a school's evaluation plan.

involved. As we collected evidence, we began to match it against the predictions of the theory of change we had articulated with them. We discussed with them how far it was substantiating that theory and what, therefore, were the implications for how they might develop their school's approach. As patterns began to emerge in the data, we looked for ways of testing them against other kinds of evidence – setting what we were told by professionals, for instance, against what the children and adults they were working with told us, or what the quantitative data seemed to be saying. As schools' FSES approaches developed, so our evaluation plans had to change too, tracking what the school was now attempting to do. In principle, this process could have continued indefinitely, but the reality was that our evaluation was time limited. After three years, however, we had for most schools a fully articulated theory of change supported by substantial amounts of evidence. This indicated whether the schools' approach was bringing about the kinds of changes for children, families and communities that the theory predicted, and therefore whether end-point outcomes (if they were not already apparent) were likely to become apparent at some point in the future.

Because the evaluation was multi-strand, we were able to consider the findings of the theory of change work alongside those of the other strands. This meant that we could compensate for the limitations of one methodology by drawing on findings from others, and that we could have more confidence in what might otherwise have been somewhat tentative findings. For instance, the detailed tracking we undertook within the theory of change approach was very good at identifying how full service provision impacted on individuals. Because we were able to combine this with a questionnaire survey and, in particular, with the NPD analysis, we were able to test how widespread these impacts were. We could also confirm that some very small differences in school performance were in fact significant for individuals and very likely to be produced by schools' full service provision. Analysed in that way, the evidence led us to a position of qualified optimism in relation to what full service and extended schools might achieve. In the next chapter, we will present that evidence in more detail. Before we do so, however, we want to consider what we learned from the evaluation process, and what its implications are for the understanding of full service and extended schools more generally.

Complex initiatives, complex evaluation

Our choice of evaluation design was based primarily on technical considerations. Put simply, we needed a way of evaluating the FSES initiative that would give us robust findings within the timescale and resources that were available to us. In designing the evaluation in the way we did, we were aware that we were deviating from more standard approaches to outcomes evaluations. We were also aware that we were exploring ways of identifying and assessing outcomes from schools that were different from those used as part of the powerful accountability mechanisms to which English schools are subject. In other words, we would not be focusing solely on short-term impacts in relation to student attainment. What we perhaps did not fully appreciate at the outset, however, was how our use of other measures and other ways of identifying impacts would change our understanding of what it means to 'evaluate' the work of schools. These changes have, we believe, implications not only for professional evaluators, but also for school leaders and for those at other levels of education systems who seek to hold schools to account. We therefore wish to spend a little time exploring three of them – changed research relationships, views of data, and understandings of causality – in some detail.

School leaders as partners

In the course of our visits to FSESs, it soon became apparent that our relationship with school leaders was very different from the traditional one of researcher and participant. It was their theories of change that shaped what full service provision meant for their school, and that we therefore sought to elicit. At the same time, since those theories were at least partially implicit, the process of elicitation was not simply a matter of asking them what they were doing and why. Rather, it was a process of dialogue in which we took what they told us and tried to give it shape, and they responded to what we produced by modifying or elaborating it. In other words, we were engaged in a process of co-construction where (as they often told us) we helped them think through what they were trying to do and, in return, they were able to give us clearer and deeper explanations of their thinking. This process was taken yet further when it came to collecting evidence as to whether the school's actions were having their intended impacts. School leaders were active partners in identifying what data might be appropriate, in overseeing its collection, and in interpreting and responding to it.

This partnership between researchers and school personnel has, we believe, some important implications for the evaluation of full service and extended schools more generally. In the English education system, judgements are typically made about schools without any consideration of what it is that school leaders are trying to achieve. The assumption is that they are simply following national imperatives and priorities. The problem with this approach, of course, is that it discounts – and, indeed, discourages – the key role leaders play in shaping the work of the school to local circumstances and needs. What our experience opens up is the possibility of acknowledging this role by making judgements through a process of dialogue. This is not simply a matter of accepting whatever school leaders say and claim at face value. As we see throughout this book, they view children, families and communities from a very particular position, and one that is not necessarily as benign as it may appear. However, the process we engaged in was one of clarifying, challenging and testing what they said. As we have suggested elsewhere (Dyson and Todd, 2010) such a process opened up the opportunity for school leaders to engage in what Argyris and Schön (1978, 1996) characterize as 'double loop learning'. In other words, they could move beyond the daily business of setting up and managing full service provision, and begin to think about its fundamental purposes and the assumptions on which it was based. Opportunities of this kind are, in our experience, all too rare in the development of full service and extended approaches in England, where, as we have seen, the emphasis has tended to be more on *what* is done than on *why* it is done.

It is, moreover, a short step from the involvement of school leaders as partners in the evaluation to their use of this approach to monitor and evaluate their own full service provision. We found that many of them were already working hard to learn about their communities and about the impacts of their actions. Some were collecting a range of data in terms of participation rates and questionnaires from participants in their activities, often in response to the accountability demands of other funding bodies and initiatives. They were also under constant pressure to keep a close eye on data relating to their students' attainments. As they did so, however, they were, as we noted earlier, sometimes at a loss as to how to use these data to identify what kinds of effects, if any, their full service provision was having. It seems to us that theory of change offers a methodology which could easily be used by schools themselves, without necessarily relying on the assistance of external evaluators. The principles on which it is based are simple, and the data it uses can often be close-to-hand for schools. Moreover, there is no reason why schools cannot use theory of change or similarly theory-based methodologies for planning their full service provision in the first place (see, for instance, Connell and Klem, 2000; W.K. Kellogg Foundation, 2004). Whilst some form of external perspective is always helpful in this process, it is by no means essential, and there is no reason why it has to be provided by university researchers.

Changing what counts as data

As we have suggested, we anticipated that using theory of change methodology would free us from an over-reliance on student attainment data. What we did not realize, however, was how much this methodology would change our view of what counts as data and how data should be used. We had not, in particular, realized how much it would foreground of the details of what had happened to individuals. In the event, our evidence base was full of case studies of young people, parents and community members, with details of their experience of an activity or service, and of the impact this had had on their lives. This was in sharp contrast to the more traditional analysis of schools and student performance data in our work on the NPD, which focused on whole school populations, and on sub-groups rather than on individuals. It meant that we were able to identify outcomes and beneficiaries that would have slipped below the radar of more conventional evaluation designs. In many cases, as we shall see in the next chapter, the work of the FSES was having transformative impacts on particular children and families, though such impacts were invisible in standard school and neighbourhood statistics.

Moreover, we also found that the cost benefit analysis was a particularly power-ful way of exploring the value of such impacts. Keeping one or two young people on track makes a minimal difference to school performance figures, and is easy to dismiss as insignificant. However, its monetary value within a cost benefit framework can be very high – quite apart from its significance for the individuals involved. This of course begs the question of what it is that is 'of value' in the work of schools. We have become accustomed (in England, at least) to seeing attainment outcomes as of value in their own right – yet what we learned was that it is also possible to value what schools do for its impacts on individual lives, and for its wider socio-economic contribution.

By the same token, 'anecdotal' evidence proved to be more significant than we had anticipated. By this we mean not just the stories we were told about and by individuals, but the accounts activity and service leaders gave us about the impacts their work was having, or the (often brief) comments that children and family or community members gave us about what services and activities had done for them. Taken individually, such anecdotes were of limited use for evaluative purposes. Taken collectively, however, and, in particular, set within a theory of change framework, they provided much more robust evidence. The point here is that theory of change methodology (at least as we used it) is not about 'proving' the effects of an initiative through statistical comparisons of measured outcomes. Nor is it about building up a rich and detailed account of a phenomenon in the way that, say, grounded theory seeks to do through the detailed analysis of qualitative data (Glaser and Strauss, 1967). Rather, it is about constructing a plausible set of hypotheses, and then testing them against the best available evidence. In this context, therefore, even 'mere anecdotes' lend weight either to the confirmation of a hypothesis or to its rejection.

Of course, working with evidence of this kind requires considerable caution so that the evaluation does not become distorted by a few 'success stories'. We found it particularly useful to be able to triangulate the data we gathered from and about individuals against the larger-scale statistical analyses, for instance. Likewise, we found it important to ask questions about 'scope' and the 'additionality' of FSES provision. For every success story we were offered, therefore, we had to ask 'how many others are there like this?', and 'would this have happened without full service provision?' We therefore had to ensure that we sought out children and adults who did not participate in activities, or for whom the school's interventions had failed, and we had to talk to professionals and community representatives outside the school who might have their own views of whether the school's interventions were helping or hindering local people.

What was very striking, however, was the extent to which school and local authority personnel undervalued the rich evidence to which they had access. In an educational culture where so much emphasis was placed on quantitative measures of student attainment, they were extremely reticent about offering other kinds of evidence or ascribing value to other kinds of data. In particular, they devalued what they saw with their own eyes and learned in the course of their routine professional activities. It seems to us, therefore, that there is an urgent need for a rebalancing of what counts as evidence if the achievements (and limitations) of full service and extended schools are to be properly identified and valued.

Rethinking causation

We are accustomed in education to working with rather straightforward models of causation – the teacher teaches and the children learn; a new teaching programme is introduced and standards of attainment rise; a new head teacher is appointed and school performance improves. Indeed, the assumption that we can identify more 'effective' actions that produce better outcomes is fundamental to efforts to 'improve' education systems, and for this reason there is a large body of research dedicated to finding 'what works' (see Hattie, 2009 for a recent, authoritative review). Theory of change evaluations, of course, rely on broadly similar assumptions, but, as we have seen, set about making explicit the links between action and outcome.

As we used theory of change methodology, this explication of causal chains began to alter our view of the relationship between action and outcome. We found, for instance, that the chains could be lengthy, and that they could interweave so that one set of actions could contribute to multiple outcomes, and any one outcome could have its origins in multiple actions. We found that, in practice, predictions about what changes would follow what actions were rarely simply confirmed or rejected. Rather, they were confirmed in some cases and under some circumstances, and disconfirmed in others. In other cases again, the jury remained out – initial changes took place as predicted, and subsequent changes seemed likely, but only if particular sets of circumstances remained in place. We therefore found ourselves dealing with a degree of indeterminacy in relation to causation. We knew *broadly* what actions were likely to produce what outcomes, but we could not be absolutely certain that we had identified all the causal pathways, nor that the pathways would be the same in every case.

To some extent, this problem could have been reduced if the evaluation had been better resourced so that we could have spent more time explicating theories of change and tracking pathways in fine detail. However, we suspect that this would not have resolved the problem entirely. As Maxwell (2004), responding to demands that education research should be more 'scientific', argues, in complex human situations, causation is never likely to be as simple and straightforwardly generalizable as our usual understandings of 'science' imply. From the point of view of full service and extended schools, this means, of course, that no-one involved in leading them – whether at institutional or system level – can be entirely certain about whether what they do will 'work' in the sense of producing its intended outcomes, or about why in any given case it has or has not 'worked'. Building a full service approach, therefore, is necessarily a somewhat exploratory and developmental business. It follows that the judgements that are made about full service and extended schools need to leave room for a degree of experimentation, and need to support the developmental process rather than punish them for a perceived failure to generate outcomes in the short term.

Towards appropriate judgements

Reviewing our experience in evaluating the FSES initiative, we believe it raises important issues about how full service and extended schools are judged – that is, about how their outcomes are assessed in formal evaluations, and about how their performance is appraised by whatever accountability mechanisms operate within a particular school system. The obvious implication is that complex and important initiatives of this kind deserve equally complex and serious evaluations. This is an issue for those governmental and non-governmental organizations which are likely to commission evaluations of initiatives they have sponsored. Our view is that there is little left to learn from small-scale and time-limited research, and that serious funding has to be put into larger-scale and, particularly, longer-term studies. Whilst the level of new funding dedicated to full service and extended school initiatives is typically not great, the overall level of resource and energy dedicated by schools is huge. Our cost benefit analysis, for instance, estimated that the monetary value of the resources dedicated by schools to their full service 'approaches' could be measured in the hundreds of thousands – if not millions – of pounds. If these sums are multiplied by the numbers of participating schools and by the many years (typically well beyond the life of the funded initiative), then the amount of funding dedicated even to a relatively well-resourced evaluation such as ours seems miniscule.

However, this is perhaps an even more significant issue for some of the other ways in which the work of full service and extended schools is judged. The intensive – and often exclusive – focus on short-term attainment outcomes in many contemporary education systems is appropriate only if raising levels of measured attainment is all that schools are expected to do. However, it seems to us self-evident that if schools begin to pursue a wider range of outcomes than those that can be measured by tests and examinations, and if they work through complex interventions, the effectiveness of their work also has to be judged in more complex ways. Specifically: they have to be judged in relation to the full range of outcomes they are pursuing; they have to be judged over a timescale adequate to allowing those outcomes to emerge; and they have to be judged in a way which takes into account the multiple forms of action in which they need to be involved, and the complex pathways from actions to outcomes.

We are far from arguing that the theory of change methodology on which we relied is the only way in which appropriate evaluations might be conducted. It has itself been criticized for being too cumbersome in practice, too inclined towards assuming that the links between action and outcome are linear, and too naïve in its assumptions about the politics shaping initiatives and their underpinning theories (see, for instance, Davies, 2004; Davies, 2005; Edwards *et al.*, 2006; Mackenzie and Blamey, 2005). More important than the technical procedures of the methods we used, however, is what we learned about the stance towards evaluation – and, more generally, towards judging schools. If the use of any particular methodology is negotiable, different understandings of evidence and causation, and a different relationship with school leaders, almost certainly are not. Only in this way might it be possible to avoid dismissing full service and extended approaches not because of their own failures, but because they are judged and evaluated in inappropriate ways.

Chapter 6

Achievements and limitations

In the previous chapter, we explored the challenges facing us in the evaluation of FSESs, and, more generally, the challenges that face all evaluators in this field. Those challenges should make us cautious about what we claim for full service and extended school approaches. The evidence we have does not always come from the most robust evaluations, and in any case is likely to be provisional and contextually bound. Nonetheless, evidence does exist, some of it at least is trustworthy, and it tends to point in broadly the same direction. Despite all the cautions and caveats, it does seem as though full service and extended schools can generate positive outcomes, and that those outcomes are particularly positive for children and families facing significant difficulties. In this chapter, therefore, we wish to report this evidence in more detail, focusing particularly on our own findings (Cummings *et al.*, 2007a) but first setting that in the context of what other researchers have found.

The international evidence

Whatever doubts there may be about the quality of the full service and extended school evidence base, the plethora of evaluative activity does seem to have produced some reasonably consistent findings. Dryfoos (2000), for instance, reports evaluation findings from 49 community school initiatives. Whilst she enters the usual caveats about the quality of the studies, she also notes that between them they report gains in 'learning and achievement, improved social behavior and healthy youth development; better family functioning and parental involvement; and, enhanced community life' (Dryfoos, 2000, p. 3).

Blank, Melaville and Shah (2003), likewise raise doubts about the quality of the evidence from the 20 initiatives which they review, yet conclude that these initiatives have produced positive outcomes in four areas:

> **Student learning**: Community school students show significant and widely evident gains in academic achievement and in essential areas of non-academic development.
>
> **Family engagement**: Families of community school students show increased

stability, communication with teachers and school involvement. Parents demonstrate a greater sense of responsibility for their children's learning success.

School effectiveness: Community schools enjoy stronger parent–teacher relationships, increased teacher satisfaction, a more positive school environment and greater community support.

Community vitality: Community schools promote better use of school buildings, and their neighborhoods enjoy increased security, heightened community pride, and better rapport among students and residents.

(Blank *et al.*, 2003, pp. 1–2, emphases in original)

In the same vein, Richardson, reviewing the field as a whole, reports a wide range of positive outcomes in relation to:

grade completion and promotion, performance on standardized tests, degree attainment, building community assets, and better use of the facility . . . commitment to lifelong learning and community service, and community pride . . . parental involvement [which] enhances student motivation and breaks down barriers between the school and community. Students whose parents are engaged in the life of the school tend to have higher achievement, demonstrate motivation, and are less apt to experience discipline problems . . . Programming can also offer parents desperately needed social and professional support as well as creative outlets.

(Richardson, 2009, pp. 57–58)

In addition to these overviews, there is also considerable evidence that some of the key components of full service and extended school approaches are associated with positive outcomes. There are many examples of this kind from England where government-sponsored and well-evaluated initiatives have developed specific forms of provision that we subsequently saw incorporated into FSESs. For instance, there is evidence that learning mentors can help raise student achievement (Ofsted, 2005; Kendall *et al.*, 2005), that multi-professional Behaviour and Education Support Teams (which often formed the basis for FSESs' multi-agency work) have positive impacts on both children and parents (Halsey *et al.*, 2005), that out of hours activities tend to produce enhanced student engagement, learning and well-being (Big Lottery Fund, 2006), and that breakfast clubs have positive impacts on family stress and parent employment decisions (Shemilt *et al.*, 2003). Evidence of this kind could be multiplied many times over, and can be supplemented by evidence from multi-strand initiatives analogous to full service and extended schools. Probably the most significant such initiative in the English context has been the Sure Start programme where multi-service hubs have been created for young children and their families. A thorough evaluation (Belsky *et al.*, 2007; National Evaluation of Sure Start, 2005; The National Evaluation of Sure Start Research Team, 2008) has identified positive outcomes in terms of better social development, more positive social behaviour and greater independence amongst children, together with more positive parenting, better access to services by families, and better home learning environments.

There seems to be a large body of evidence, then, which suggests that full service and extended school approaches are likely to produce many of the outcomes their leaders and advocates claim for them. Nonetheless, there are two caveats which should immediately be entered. First, although the evidence suggests that these approaches are very likely to be ameliorative in their effects, it is difficult to claim that they are in any sense transformative, at least at the school or area population level. Typically, evaluations report apparently impressive improvements for children and families across a range of indicators (see, for instance, Coalition for Community Schools, 2009, for a recent review). However, the improvements often relate to low-performing groups of students achieving more highly than they were doing previously, or students in full service and extended schools doing better than those in other kinds of schools, or families accessing more services than they had done hitherto. It is difficult to find evidence that any improvements are sustained, or that they transfer from specific indicators to better life chances overall, or that they could not have been obtained by means other than full service provision. Above all, it is difficult to find evidence that improvements are so great, so sustained and so generalized that the effects of any social and economic disadvantages experienced by children and families are entirely negated.

Second, there are strong suggestions in the evidence base that the impacts of full service and extended schools are variable. In other words, some schools have some impacts on some indicators for some children and adults, but there is no guarantee that they 'work' in all circumstances. The evaluation of an Australian full service schools programme, for instance, concludes that it 'had a significant impact on the educational opportunities of at risk young people and has demonstrated value for money' (Szirom et al., 2001, p. 2). On closer inspection, however, this definition of success seems to allow for up to 15 per cent of its target group of students dropping out of school, up to half of participating schools reporting no significant changes in their practices and procedures, a third of schools reporting no improvement in community relations, and so on. Similarly, the evaluation of the Scottish New Community Schools pilot (Sammons et al., 2003) found improvements in attainment outcomes in participating schools – but no greater than those obtained by schools outside the initiative. A relatively large scale evaluation of after-school programmes (usually a significant component of full service and extended schools) likewise concludes that participating students were:

> no more likely to have higher academic achievement, no less likely to be in self-care, more likely to engage in some negative behaviors, and experience mixed effects on developmental outcomes relative to students who were not randomly assigned to attend the centers.
>
> (James-Burdumy et al., 2005, p. xii)

Again, it would be easy to multiply examples of this kind. There is, of course, no inherent problem with impacts that are variable. Where impacts are positive, they are worth having, and there is always the possibility that we can learn 'what works' and ensure that it becomes more widespread. Likewise, there is no inherent problem with impacts that are 'only' ameliorative. As Riddell and Tett (2004) argue in respect of the somewhat disappointing outcomes from Scottish New Community Schools:

> Even if a given initiative proves relatively powerless to bring about major social change, this does not mean that its contribution is worthless. In this case there were a number of achievements but they were not *transformative* in the sense that social exclusion was tackled or social justice enhanced. Nevertheless they were *sustaining* for the schools that participated in that they were able to implement a number of initiatives that led to modest improvements in the lives of staff, pupils and parents.
>
> (Riddell and Tett, 2004, p. 227, emphasis in original)

Nonetheless, it does seem that we need to be careful not to be seduced by the breathless tone adopted by some advocates for full service and extended schools. It seems very likely that such schools do indeed have positive impacts, but that these impacts take the form of 'modest improvements' and 'sustaining' rather than 'transformative' changes. It follows that, as we argued in the previous chapter, we need evaluation methodologies that are sufficiently sensitive to detect these impacts and to give them their due weight. The extent to which the methodologies we used in our evaluation of the FSES initiative were able to achieve this began to emerge in the school case studies we presented in chapter three. There we saw, in particular, the kinds of impacts that schools were having on individual students and families – impacts that are often difficult to assess in studies that search exclusively for large-scale statistical effects. In the remainder of this chapter, therefore, we wish to explore that evidence in more detail. Overall, our conclusions confirm the positive findings of the international evidence on full service and extended schools. However, they amplify and elaborate that evidence in ways which both give us greater confidence in what such schools can achieve, and also alert us to what might need to be done for those achievements to become even more significant.

The FSES evaluation: evidence of impact

In line with the international evidence, our evaluation of FSESs suggested that they were capable of generating positive outcomes for children and young people, families, communities and schools. At the whole population level – in other words, what happened to schools' students as a whole and to the families and communities they served – our analyses of quantitative indicators suggested the presence of positive effects, but ones that were somewhat limited and uncertain. When our theory of change methodology enabled us to track FSESs' impacts at the individual and family level, however, we found a different picture. Here we encountered children and adults for whom the services and activities offered by schools had made a significant difference and where, in a few cases at least, it might not be an exaggeration to say that the impact had indeed been transformative.

Our findings are reported in detail in our final evaluation report (Cummings *et al.*, 2007a). In the remainder of this chapter, we summarize what we learned from the various strands of our evaluation, beginning with a brief account of our analyses of the National Pupil Database (NPD) and our cost benefit analysis, then turning in more detail to report the findings of our theory of change evaluation. All references to institutions and individuals are anonymized. Where names are given these are pseudonyms.

Impacts on school-level attainment outcomes

All the FSESs with which we worked saw improved attainment outcomes for their students as a key aim of their provision. The analysis of the NPD, which we described briefly in the previous chapter, was the obvious way of testing for such impacts. However, it produced mixed results. We were not, for instance, able to identify an FSES 'effect' on overall attainments in participating schools. There was no evidence, in other words, that being educated in an FSES enabled the majority of pupils to attain more highly than they would if they were educated in other schools. The best we could say was that neither was there evidence of any overall negative effect. This was important given that some critics at the time (see, for instance, Brookes, 2006) were arguing that developing extended provision would distract schools from their 'core business' of raising attainment. In the same way, when we attempted to analyse a range of neighbourhood statistics for the areas served by FSESs, we could find no evidence for any impacts. Whilst there are all sorts of caveats about the sensitivity of the indicators that we had at our disposal, the reality is that we were not able to find evidence from these analyses that schools had as yet produced the kinds of area transformation at which some of them, at least, aimed.

However, a more fine-grained analysis began to hint at something different. In some individual schools, there were quite dramatic gains in student attainment, as well as reductions in absence and behavioural problems. The difficulty in interpreting these changes is that, taken on their own, they did not show whether the improvements were due to FSES status or to a range of other changes that were typically taking place in schools – and in any case we could certainly have found schools outside the initiative where improvements were equally dramatic. Overall, however, there were some 'rather limited' indications from our NPD analysis to show that the gaps in attainment between the more vulnerable groups in FSESs (those identified as having special educational needs and/or those entitled to free school meals) and their peers might be a little narrower than in other schools. A separate analysis undertaken as part of the evaluation by government statisticians also suggested that levels of attainment were rising faster in FSESs than in their nearest comparator schools – though the matching of comparator groups was not comprehensive. Such findings on their own are far from conclusive, but they are nonetheless encouraging rather than otherwise.

Impacts on children, young people and their families

Given what we have said in previous chapters about the complexities of evaluating full service and extended schools using standard input-outcome measures, we were not entirely surprised at these ambiguous findings. However, this ambiguity did not match what many school leaders believed to be the impacts of their work. Responses to the school questionnaire suggested that half thought that full service provision had had significant positive impacts on families, on children's personal, social and health outcomes, and on school ethos. More specifically, most thought it had had some kind of impact on one or more of: the achievements of students; the engagement of children in learning; supporting families at risk; parent involvement in school; learning opportunities for the community; and the quality of life of the local community. Responses to the student questionnaires lent some support to these claims. Those in FSESs were more likely than their peers elsewhere to agree that their school tried to help them, their parents and local people with their problems, and that parents and teachers talked to each other often. Likewise, parents of children in FSESs were more likely than others to feel that the school made them welcome, and that it offered help to them and other local residents.

The strongest evidence for impacts of this kind, however, came from the work we did in trying to substantiate or otherwise schools' theories of change. In the course of this work we unearthed many individual cases like those we described in chapter three, which indicated that full service provision could have significant impacts on children facing difficulties. We saw there, for instance, how Simon was kept on track by Clark School, despite having been excluded from other schools in the area. We were offered a similar example in a primary school which had established a team of professionals to deliver a range of social and educational supports to parents. At the time we visited the school, this team had been accessed by at least a third of all families with children on roll. As a result there were many individual stories of how this support had helped families to maintain stability and had had significant impacts on children's learning in school. For example, Kevin, we were told:

> joined us two years ago from [another school]. The child's father had died and he'd had erratic attendance at his old school . . . He was doing OK at school, but then he stopped coming in and Mum came into school at her wit's end, not knowing what to do. Within 24 hours we had support in place and Social Care and Health supported the child who is now settled in school. Over a very short period of time the support kicked in and he is now settled in school and will be a very successful learner.

A further example came from St James' College, whose provision we described in chapter three. Part of that provision took the form of a multi-disciplinary 'inclusion team' to work with young people in difficulties. Here one of the team members describes her work with Susie, who:

was referred in year 9. Her behaviour in school was aggressive towards teachers and staff. She wasn't staying in lessons. She was a substance misuser and had outside issues with boyfriends and relationships with other young people. There was no family liaison. She was disaffected with school and at risk of exclusion. When I spoke to her I found she had very little self-esteem and she was involved in substance misuse. So the work I did involved home visits so parents were involved and I did self esteem and anger management sessions [with the pupil] and linked in with the inclusion team so she could do 4 GCSEs [national examinations] . . . and I supported her to and from her work placement. I also referred her to the substance misuse worker who comes into school . . . The inclusion team and I got her a taster course at a FE [further education] college in hairdressing and beauty so her timetable was a flexible package, so she did this and had sessions to do her GCSEs. We picked her up in Year 9 and did preventative work to try and get her back in class but it wasn't working, so in Year 10 I arranged with the school the work placement. I also showed her around different FE colleges to remove any pre-judgments. When she left Year 11 she came here [the school] to apply to do [a vocational qualification] in early years. Her attendance has been brilliant and now she is looking to work in social care and I've linked her with the social worker [in the FSES] to get a grounding in the job . . . Before this she was being less abusive with staff and said she wanted to come back to school and attend regularly . . . [Without support] I don't think she would have finished school. She had no aspirations and wanted to work in the local caf[é]. It's really boosted her self-esteem and she is now thinking of helping other young people that she says 'were like me'. It's so great when it goes like this. It's the multi-agency staff that's given this input.

As we have seen in earlier chapters, FSES leaders typically articulated theories of change which predicted that extended services and activities would help overcome the multiple problems in students' lives – conceptualized as 'barriers to learning' – would enable students to re-engage with the learning process, and in turn would enable them to achieve, gain accreditation, and so improve their life chances. The evidence from individual cases, such as those of Simon, Kevin and Susie, lent support to these predictions. Moreover, there was a recurrent pattern in how schools managed to impact on their students' trajectories. The immediate cause of change in these young people seemed to consist in contact with supportive adults. Often these were not teachers working in the school's core teaching and learning provision, but other adults working within the school's full service provision. Crucially, these adults, unconstrained by the demands of classroom management, were well-placed to identify the range of difficulties in children's lives, and, above all, to respond to children tolerantly, positively, and as individuals. They were then able to work with other professionals and with the child to remove or ameliorate these difficulties.

In the same way, FSESs were well-placed to work with families. As schools tackled students' difficulties, they became aware of how far those difficulties might be related to family circumstances, and had personnel on hand who could make contact with parents. Alternatively, parents themselves might self-refer to the various support workers based in school. The school was then able to put in place some sort of family support, using its own staff, or linking the family to other agencies, or setting up some sort of support network. As a result, families such as Kevin's that were 'at their wit's end' began to find ways of managing their problems. The adults became more confident and more outward looking, and often some kind of virtuous circle was established where the parents' increased confidence was reflected in the stability of the child, and the child's stability was reflected in the increased confidence of the parents. Interactions of this kind were evident throughout our data.

Just as the difficulties of parents and children impacted on one another, so as in the cases of Simon, Kevin and Susie, learning difficulties interacted with problems of substance misuse, emotional instability, bereavement, truancy, and criminality. Moreover, this was true not only of extreme cases such as these. FSESs often provided open access services, such as drop-in health clinics or curriculum sessions, or self-referrals to support workers. The evidence we gathered suggested that these forms of provision helped prevent problems escalating to crisis point and, crucially, kept potentially vulnerable students engaged with the school. Something as simple as the presence of a nurse in school, for instance, meant that low level health problems could be dealt with immediately without students needing to take time off school.

Impacts on adults, communities and the school

Some of the schools in our sample held a theory of change which envisaged them making impacts on a wider scale than on students and their families. If, they reasoned, the achievements and well-being of children and young people were shaped principally by their families, they were also influenced by the areas where they lived. In particular, the cultural norms and values of people in local communities were important influences on children and families, and these in turn were shaped by the opportunities and material conditions under which people lived. These schools therefore set about impacting on all of these factors.

We found strong evidence that FSESs could have impacts on adults that were as significant as their impacts on children and young people. There was a common pattern of how these impacts took place – one that we have already witnessed in chapter three, in the case of Jenny at Beresford School. Typically, adults would find themselves in 'dead end' situations. They would often have left school at the first opportunity and with few qualifications, have moved in and out of unstable, low-skilled and low-paid employment, and, in the case of women, would have given up work when they had children. In time, some of them told us, this drained their confidence and they felt there was no way of improving their circumstances. However, when they began to engage with the school – either because their children went there or because the school was offering some attractive leisure opportunities – they found themselves welcomed, offered help with practical problems, and encouraged to take up adult learning opportunities. For some of them, this led to accreditation, or to voluntary work in the school, or to employment elsewhere.

Some of these cases were dramatic. For instance, one head teacher, whose school offered adult learning courses and hosted a multi-agency team, told us how:

> with one family, the single mum had a history of drugs and she used to prostitute and concerns were raised. [The social worker] went [to the home] to do some investigatory work. The children didn't have a bed, never mind a bedtime or structure . . . [The social worker] was *this* close to having the children removed. This woman got lots of support from [the social worker]. This woman now attends courses at the school. She dresses like she values herself and is ready to learn. Her children are ready for school now and they have a proper bed. How do you measure that? It's absolutely brilliant!

Others might be less dramatic, but were equally significant for the individuals concerned:

> One young lady came to join the craft group. She had poor health and depression. She did really well in the craft group and began to help others, so this was a boost to her self-esteem. She decided to become a volunteer helper and now she is employed here. She has done all the IT training and her confidence has grown incredibly.

The most powerful testimony, however, was from the adults themselves. As a group of adult learners in one school told us:

> It wakes your brain up, especially if you have been a stay at home mum for so long and I've grown in confidence.
> I left school with no certificates or qualifications so to get these [shows a file of certificates] it is great.
> I passed English and Maths [at the school] and now I've moved on to do my GCSE in English at [a local college].
> I'm the only man here and the helpful thing is I can always get help here. I'm not afraid to ask here. I've been made to feel that I can ask. I never listened at school and to think I've come here 6 years after I finished school and I've learnt more here.

In this way, the most significant effects were in enabling people to move from a position where they had no qualifications and very limited prospects, to one where doors were beginning to open for them. Where adults were facing problems, FSESs were able to offer them information, advice and support that were otherwise simply not available – or, at least, that they would not feel confident enough to access. Often, adults were encouraged to support each other rather than becoming dependent on the guidance of professionals. As one young mother told us:

> You are normally stuck in a flat. This gets you out and you can get advice here on benefits and how to find work. You are also with people the same age who might

say, 'have you tried this'. We give support to one another and you get support from [the staff] also.

Very frequently, therefore, people participating in adult learning provision told us that they had been reluctant to become engaged in learning, but that the school staff had encouraged them, that they had taken some first tentative steps, and that eventually they had gained the confidence to take more challenging, accredited courses. As this process brought adults closer to the labour market, it helped that FSESs themselves were significant employers of local people – in one school, over 80 per cent of non-teaching staff were recruited from the area – and thus were able to offer relatively 'safe' ways of re-entering employment.

Many school leaders anticipated that, in time, these impacts on individuals would accumulate into impacts on whole communities. They hoped that changing the outlook of individual adults and generating a flow of positively minded young people into the community would eventually bring about some kind of wider cultural shift, so that dispirited and dysfunctional (as they saw them) norms and values would become a thing of the past. In the meantime, they tried to help that shift along by developing the capacity of local people to support each other, and by engaging their students in various leadership activities in preparation for their future role in their communities. In a few cases, where local communities were characterized by a structure of clear cultural groups with identified leaders, they might be able to have more direct impacts. For instance, the head of one school serving a multi-ethnic area told us how the school had played a part in defusing inter-ethnic tensions both within and beyond the school's boundaries:

> a few years ago we had a lot of problems with Afro-Caribbean street culture and middle eastern, Afghani tensions . . . Two years after, when we had the [place name] Afghani heavies and things started to build up, and that was all defused by [the FSES coordinator] contacting different agencies. We got them in to school . . . The Afghani mentor was absolutely crucial at the time . . . and importantly the elders from that community . . . came into the school and talked to these boys in their own language and just turned the situation around, and having the community in our school, the same values that we were trying to encourage, it just worked like a dream.

Certainly, FSESs were able to show that their outward-facing stance had an effect on how they were perceived by local communities. Many of them described a situation before the start of the FSES initiative where they did badly on standard performance measures (of overall attainment, attendance and exclusions), where there was some breakdown of trust between the school and local people, and where many families were opting to send their children to other local schools. However, over half of the schools responding to our questionnaire survey believed that making full service provision had enhanced their standing in the community. In some cases, the changes were dramatic, with schools whose survival was threatened reporting a sharp upturn in student recruitment, whilst other schools reported significantly increased participation in activities organized by the school, and increased attendance at parents' consultation evenings.

Costs and benefits

The cost benefit analysis (CBA) which formed a part of our evaluation was intended to find an alternative way to gauge the impact of FSESs' work. Whereas most educational evaluations rely heavily on measures of student attainment to determine what difference an initiative has made, CBA, as we saw in the previous chapter, effectively asks what society invests in and gains from an initiative, attaching monetary values to both. Our analysis showed some interesting – perhaps surprising – outcomes. First, the costs were very high because schools made use of resources that were funded from outside the initiative – notably, the time of their own staff and of staff from other agencies – so that the real cost of their provision went well beyond any additional monies they received or raised. A number of schools, for instance, deployed resources worth over £1,000 per student per year. In one case, the overall annual cost of provision was over £2 million, and even primary schools were likely to be deploying resources worth well over £200,000 per year.

By the same token, the monetary value of benefits was also generally high – perhaps higher than expected. Schools were pressed to identify not just individual cases where their provision had made a difference, but the numbers of students and adults for whom these impacts had occurred – and, so far as possible, we checked these claims against other evidence. One secondary FSES, for instance, was able to provide some kind of evidence that, amongst other things, its provision enabled 21 students each year to gain higher examination grades, and reduced teenage births by 5, cases of sexually transmitted diseases by 14, cases of alcohol and drug abuse by 25, and cases of smoking by 10. Such impacts are clearly important for the individuals concerned, but they also indicate important socio-economic benefits, since there would otherwise have to be significant investment in health services and welfare benefits as these young people progressed into and through adulthood. Looked at in this way, the lifetime value of even a small improvement in examination results was over £160,000, and the value of each avoided teenage birth was over £65,000. Not surprisingly, therefore, the total value of all of the reported benefits in this school was very high indeed – over £5.5 million. Even in less dramatic cases, values were well over £1 million, and were often double that figure.

The calculation of these costs and benefits involved a good deal of estimation (though if anything the methods we had to use meant that there was a chance that benefits were under-estimated). Our overall conclusion, however, was twofold. First, that benefits tended to outweigh costs – and sometimes quite significantly so. Second, that benefits tended to accrue to the most disadvantaged individuals, so that there was a redistributive effect in the work of FSESs.

Additionality and scope

Asking schools about the numbers of children and adults on whom their work impacted was important not just for the cost benefit analysis, but also for determining the *scope* of FSESs' impacts. We had good evidence of powerful impacts on individuals – but were these simply isolated cases, or was full service provision making a difference to large numbers of people? What we found, in general terms, was that the most significant impacts were restricted to a minority of the school population, and a small minority of the adult population of local communities. Typically, FSESs could make most difference to children and adults facing significant difficulties, in support of whom they could deploy relatively high-powered individual interventions. On the other hand, given that schools were serving highly disadvantaged populations, these minorities were nonetheless quite large ones, and the success rates in terms of positive outcomes were high. As we saw in the figures quoted earlier and again in chapter three, it was not unusual for schools to be working more-or-less intensively not just with a few individuals, but with scores of students and adults. It was, for instance, not uncommon for schools to report that they were working in this way with some 10 per cent of their population in any school year, that in many cases families would be involved, and that it was rare for there to be no positive outcomes from these interventions.

In terms of more widespread impacts, however, these tended to be of a different order of magnitude. Most FSESs offered less intensive services and activities that involved a high proportion of their student population and relatively large numbers of local people. Typically, these took the form of group activities – out of hours learning activities for students, perhaps, or leisure classes for adults, or community arts events. They were certainly not without impact, and we spoke to many participants who expressed their enjoyment of such activities, and the more positive attitude this gave them towards the school and, in some cases, to themselves. However, they did not report the same sort of transformative effects that were associated with intensive individual interventions.

In assessing all of these impacts, we also considered the issue of *additionality* – in other words, the extent to which similar impacts would have materialized anyway, even if the school had not offered full service provision. This was difficult to gauge since it involved exploring with informants what might have been the case, or, more concretely, what had been the case before the school developed as an FSES. Nonetheless, a pattern began to emerge. For the most part, the provision offered by schools did not simply replace existing provision offered elsewhere, and there was little evidence that other agencies reduced their provision in response to what the school was doing. On the contrary, what seemed to be happening was that there was some absolute increase in the level of provision available locally. This was because the school appointed new staff to work with children, families and adults, whilst other agencies relocated their services on the school site where they were more easily accessed by their intended users. This was particularly the case with the various drop-in clinics, advice centres, and mentoring schemes that sprang up in FSESs. These may or may not have been available previously in community settings, but it was clear that both students and adults had simply tended not to access them until they were close at hand, and until school staff were able to encourage them to take advantage of what was on offer.

What became particularly evident was that full service provision was working in what one head teacher called 'the zone in-between'. What he meant by this was that there had long been a gap between the strictly limited amount of child and family support that schools could offer, and the even more strictly limited services that other agencies could offer. The latter in particular were often only able to respond to crisis cases and their provision was rationed through cumbersome referral procedures. By expanding the school's own capacity, he argued, and by persuading other agencies to work in and with the school, FSESs were beginning to fill this gap. Because they worked closely with children and their families on a daily basis, and because they did not rely on formal referral processes, they were able to intervene long before problems reached crisis point. As they did this, what they discovered was that there was a 'pool of unmet need' in disadvantaged areas. Children, families and adults, like many of those whose stories we have told here and in chapter three, faced problems that were significant in terms of their life chances and well-being, but which never quite triggered the standard referral processes, or which, if they did, produced short-term crisis responses, leaving underlying problems unresolved. It was often the schools, therefore, which could work most effectively with such children and families, staying in close contact with them over extended periods, and offering them clear, if undramatic, pathways out of their difficulties.

In this respect, the multi-strand nature of FSES provision seems to have been important. Children and families often did not face a single problem so much as a interacting clusters of difficulties, which crossed the boundaries of traditional service provision. One primary school behaviour worker gave us a typical example of such a situation, and described how the school had responded:

> One particular boy was constantly in trouble. He had low level, ongoing issues of behaviour and was being sent home at lunch times but this was aggravating the situation rather than helping. So we sent him to breakfast club and it transpired that as the youngest in the family he was getting himself up and wasn't always getting in on time or thinking about breakfast. He is attending now and eating. CAMHS [Child and Adolescent Mental Health Services] are involved through the school nurse and [there is also] Children's Forum [a local initiative to elicit and act in response to young people's views]. Mum has reported that he is better behaved at home and he is definitely better in school, and because he is being praised every day and people are showing interest, this is helping his self esteem. I've also got a list of activities that mother is interested in and I'll ask [the FSES coordinator] to accompany her to these clubs so she does not feel intimidated.

The interactions here are clear – the boy's troublesome behaviour in school, his equally troublesome behaviour at home, an apparently chaotic family, a mother lacking in confidence, an inadequate diet. Equally clear is the way that the school can call on a range of provision to tackle this situation – the interventions of the behaviour worker, the breakfast club, the nurse, the links with the Children's Forum, the adult learning provision. We had many examples of such multi-strand interventions in FSESs. Significantly, however, it was not possible to find anything equivalent in comparator schools that had not developed a full array of extended provision.

Some conclusions and caveats

Many of our findings about outcomes from FSESs support the positive picture that emerges from the international literature on full service and extended schools. Such schools could and did make positive differences to the lives and life chances of the children, families and adults whom they served. Some of those differences were relatively small, but were widespread across school and (to a lesser extent) area populations. However, in the case of individuals and families facing significant difficulties, the impacts of full service provision could be major, even transformative. The numbers of such cases were not great, but in schools serving disadvantaged populations, neither were they restricted to a very few individuals. Moreover, when the value of the 'benefits' generated by FSESs was calculated in monetary terms, it turned out to be high and to outweigh the costs of investment in that provision. From a purely economic standpoint, full service provision turned out to be a good way to spend public money and to use public resources.

There is more good news. Although the effort involved in developing a full service or extended school is undoubtedly considerable, there is no evidence that this impacts negatively on the school's core mission of raising its students' educational achievements. On the contrary, although the evidence is far from conclusive, we found some indications that such schools *might* do better than schools which do not develop full service provision, and that attainment gaps *may* be a little narrower in FSESs. Certainly, we found plenty of evidence that individual students who might otherwise achieve very little tend to do better as a result of the wider services and activities offered by the school.

Overall, the theories of change articulated by FSES leaders tended to be substantiated rather than otherwise. Those leaders believed that they could not, in the context of the disadvantaged populations they served, make much more progress even with the limited business of raising students' achievements unless they offered a wider range of services and activities. They believed that they needed to tackle the 'barriers to learning' faced by their students, and that this might also involve tackling issues in their families and communities. They believed that establishing an array of services and activities in and around the school would enable them to tackle these issues, so that students achieved more highly. At the same time, students, their families and local communities would enjoy greater well-being and enhanced life chances. In all of the schools we studied, it was possible to identify multiple cases where the assumptions underpinning such theories were proved to be correct. In other words, there were children, families and adults doing much better as a result of the interventions marshalled by FSESs than they otherwise might have done.

In terms of the relationship between socio-economic disadvantage and educational outcomes, this is an important finding. It suggests that this relationship is not a deterministic one. Experiencing disadvantage may well increase the risks of children doing badly in education and going on to face more limited life chances, but the sorts of activities and services available in full service and extended schools can at the very least ameliorate these risks. This is an issue to which we shall return in the next chapter. Moreover, although the overall costs of these services and interventions are high, the marginal costs are not. For the most part, as we saw in chapter three, FSESs called on *relatively* little additional funding. The bulk of the cost of provision came in the form of resources that were already funded and available. The key, therefore, lay in using those resources in a different way, making them more accessible to children, families and adults, and creating possibilities for coordinated action and mutual reinforcement.

It is at this point, however, where we need to enter some caveats about the achievements of full service and extended schools in general, and of FSESs in particular. For all our attempts to consider issues of additionality and scope, it is in the discrepancy between their undoubtedly positive impacts on individuals and their much less certain impacts on social and educational disadvantage as a whole that these schools' achievements begin to appear problematic. For instance, although FSESs undoubtedly made a difference to some individuals and families, there were other cases where impacts failed to materialize. In one school which had established a multi-disciplinary family support team, the FSES coordinator expressed the reality somewhat ruefully:

> We thought if only we got this team together, we could cut out all problems. We aren't the answer to all of life's problems . . . We have seen very definite and very positive impact on families. We've seen transformation and empowerment with many families, but there are a couple of families where the problems are so ingrained and progress is slower.

Taking this observation a step further, there were almost certainly many children, families and adults in the areas served by these schools who never came to their attention: children in the school whose difficulties were hidden; those who attended other nearby schools without full service provision; families and adults without school age children. Even for those with whom the school worked successfully, there was no guarantee that interventions would be continued once the child left the school. It may be that what FSESs were able to provide was enough to alter the long-term trajectories of some students and families, but it seems equally likely that some, at least, would succumb to their difficulties as they moved beyond the supportive environments that their schools had created.

There are further caveats to add about the community impacts of FSESs. It seemed reasonable to suppose that, if the work of these schools could be sustained over time, the kind of wider cultural changes at which many of them aimed might eventually materialize. However, there were two problems here. First, it was not at all clear that their work would in fact be sustained. The FSES initiative itself lasted only three years, with no guarantee of funding beyond that point. In any case, we found in other work (Crowther *et al.*, 2003) that the commitment of schools to full service and extended approaches depends heavily on the attitudes and values of their head teachers – and that head teachers frequently move on. We might add that, in the turbulent policy climate in England, schools too 'move on' frequently, and that those serving disadvantaged areas are particularly likely to be closed, merged, taken over or re-launched. At least two of the 17 schools with which we worked most closely, for instance, have already ceased to exist in their original form.

Second, although FSESs were making strenuous efforts to tackle the consequences of disadvantage in the communities they served, we saw much less evidence that they were able to do much to tackle the material realities or the underlying causes of disadvantage. Overwhelmingly, their work was with the skills, attitudes and values of individuals and families. They could and did enable some of them to become more employable, and, in some cases, to become a little more confident in tackling community problems. However, they were in no position to reduce poverty as such, nor to generate employment (beyond the limited opportunities they themselves could offer), nor to secure better housing, transport links, wages or benefits.

At the heart of these limitations was the nature of the FSES initiative as a short-term, school-centred and essentially non-strategic attempt to intervene in the relationship between social and educational disadvantage. It created a flurry of activity around individual schools, but did not lock those schools either into any coordinated network of local provision, or into any wider and longer-term strategy. In this context, FSESs were able to do much that was ameliorative – and even transformative – for individuals, but they had no way of impacting on underlying social and economic conditions. It seems to us that, in this respect at least, the FSES initiative is typical of most developments of full service and extended schools across the world. Even if we accept the positive evidence from evaluations at face value, we have to set it in this wider context. Whatever a full service school here or a community school there can achieve for the children, families and adults with whom they engage, this is likely to mean little without more sustained and wide-ranging strategies to tackle disadvantage.

This realization could easily lead to pessimistic conclusions about the value of full service and extended school approaches. On their own, and in the form they have traditionally taken, they achieve little more than limited local improvements. However, there is a more optimistic perspective. Full service and extended schools can and do make a difference to people's lives. The policy developments in England subsequent to the launch of the FSES initiative – the Every Child Matters agenda and the requirement for all schools to offer access to extended services – suggest, moreover, that more strategic approaches are indeed possible. It may be that full service and extended school initiatives as we have known them in the past are not so much a dead end as the starting point for more ambitious and more productive developments. In the next chapter, therefore, we consider these issues in more detail, reviewing the limitations of full service and extended schools in their current form, but also exploring the new possibilities that we believe they open up.

Chapter 7

Rethinking full service and extended schools

The evidence we presented in the previous chapter suggested grounds for optimism about what full service and extended school approaches might achieve. That optimism is tempered, however, by the lack of any clear indication that schools working in this way can mount a credible attack on the deep-rooted problem of social disadvantage and its apparently intractable link to poor educational outcomes. It is weakened still further by the limitations of the available evidence base, and by the problematic issues that we have raised throughout this book. We saw in chapter four, for instance, how uncertain the place of full service and extended schools seems to be in many education systems – how they frequently appear as localized, occasional and time-limited initiatives, dependent on grants and project funding, and relying on partnerships with agencies and services over which they have no control. We saw, moreover, how many of their attempts at 'boundary-crossing' were hamstrung by lack of clarity as to what they were supposed to achieve, by an absence of effective policy support and, particularly, by inappropriate accountability processes. In the first two chapters, we saw how underlying this were views that changed over time, across school systems and between initiatives as to what full service and extended schools are for and how they are supposed to work. Here and in the case studies we presented in chapter three, we saw how, in the midst of this uncertainty, a 'dominant rationale' has emerged which views such schools as a means of supporting children, families and adults in disadvantaged circumstances. Yet, we also saw that this rationale is highly problematic, and that the focus on disadvantage runs the risk of stereotyping and further marginalizing the very people these schools claim to be trying to help.

In the light of all this, the claim that such schools embody 'an idea whose time has come' (Full-service Schools Roundtable, p. 181) may seem somewhat premature. We might well ask what, precisely, that 'idea' is. That there has been a flurry of activity around encouraging schools to set up additional services is beyond doubt. That this activity has had some positive – albeit modest – outcomes also seems clear. There is currently, however, no agreed, credible and fully thought-through rationale on which the development of full service and extended schools might be based – much less any model of how such schools might operate to maximum effect. If, therefore, the undoubtedly impressive level of activity in this field is ever to amount to anything more than a 'flurry', it seems to us that any future developments will have to be based on much more solid foundations than has typically been the case in the past. It will be necessary to be much clearer than before what are the problems to which full service and extended schools are the solution, what it is, precisely, that they are expected to achieve, and what is the wider context – in terms of education policy and, more generally, in terms of building and sustaining viable communities and societies – in which their work is to be located. Put in the terms we have used elsewhere in this book, such schools need to be based on an explicit, coherent, and wide-ranging theory of change.

Our view is that the development of theories of this kind can, in the final analysis, only be done in context. What full service and extended schools are for and how they should work depends to a significant extent on where they are located, what are the social realities of those locales, and how other services are configured there. Decisions, therefore, cannot be made in the light of some decontextualized blueprint. Perhaps more important, the formulation of such theories needs to raise questions of fundamental educational aims and social values. This means that it calls for an open debate amongst the stakeholders in each situation – whether they be the leaders of an individual school and the people they seek to serve, or the leaders of a national government and the people who elect them. We therefore make no pretence that we can offer a ready-made rationale for full service and extended schools that will fit all circumstances. On the other hand, the work we have done with such schools in recent years and, more particularly, the questions we have raised in this book mean that we may have something helpful to contribute to the essentially local debates that, in our view, need now to take place. In particular, we may be able to set out some of the issues that need to be explored, and offer some tools that might be useful in thinking those issues through.

In the remainder of this chapter, this is what we set out to do. We begin by revisiting the account we gave in earlier chapters of the policy context in which the recent interest in full service and extended schools has arisen. We ask what it is about that context that makes such schools seem an attractive option, and how in fact they might help resolve some of the policy problems that currently seem intractable. We go on to consider what tackling those problems might involve, what conditions need to be in place to make such efforts effective, and how some of the pitfalls into which previous attempts have fallen might now be avoided. Finally, we move beyond seeing full service and extended schools as a response to presenting problems, and consider how they might become part of wider efforts to provide good education, and to build thriving communities in the context of a healthy society.

The current situation

In chapter one, we saw how full service and extended schools have emerged in particular policy contexts, and how ideas about what they are and are for have changed over time. If, therefore, we are to build firm foundations for such schools in the future, we need to be clear what the current policy context is, what problems it contains, and what it is that such schools might contribute to the solution of those problems.

The kinds of education policy changes we described as having taken place in England over recent years are by no means unique amongst industrial (or, some would say, post-industrial) countries. The reality is that education systems in such countries across the world have been subject to repeated and fundamental reforms over the past two or three decades. Policy makers have been faced with a restructuring of the global economy which has reduced the importance of heavy manufacturing in the most industrialized countries, and has increased the role played by advanced technology and service industries. As a result, they have come to the conclusion that their countries cannot compete by selling unskilled labour cheaply, and instead have to base their prosperity on the skills and knowledge of their populations. In many respects, England, as an early industrializing, early de-industrializing country, is simply leading the pack. As a review of the skills needs of the UK economy put it:

> In the 19th Century, the UK had the natural resources, the labour force and the inspiration to lead the world into the Industrial Revolution. Today, we are witnessing a different type of revolution. For developed countries who cannot compete on natural resources and low labour costs, success demands a more service-led economy and high value-added industry.
>
> In the 21st Century, our natural resource is our people – and their potential is both untapped and vast. Skills will unlock that potential. The prize for our country will be enormous – higher productivity, the creation of wealth and social justice.
>
> The alternative? Without increased skills, we would condemn ourselves to a lingering decline in competitiveness, diminishing economic growth and a bleaker future for all.
>
> (Leitch, 2006, p. 1)

The key to 'unlocking the potential' of the nation's people – and hence to economic prosperity, and social well-being – has been seen as being education. It is in this context that former British Prime Minister Tony Blair's famous statement, that the three priorities for his government would be 'education, education and education' (Blair, 1996), should be seen. At the same time, the growth of international assessments such as PISA (OECD, no date) have made governments acutely aware of how the performance of their education systems match up (or, in some cases, fail to match up) to those of their economic competitors. Many affluent countries seem to have come to the conclusion that theirs are simply not fit for purpose in the context of a new, skills- and knowledge-based economy. Even where schools have not been seen as totally dysfunctional, the historical emphasis on a liberal education and personal development has come to seem ill-suited to a highly competitive global economy where what matters are the skills individuals can bring to the labour market. At the very beginning of the economic restructuring process, one of Blair's predecessors, James Callaghan, bemoaned the imbalance in the education system between the development of the individual and the needs of the economy. 'There is', he concluded 'no virtue in producing socially well-adjusted members of society who are unemployed because they do not have the skills' (Callaghan, 1976).

The focus on education, therefore, has rapidly transformed itself into a focus on a particular *type* of education – one in which the mastery of skills and knowledge has been all important, and in which that mastery has had to be demonstrated through rather narrowly constructed measures of attainment. So, as we saw earlier, Tony Blair's 'education, education and education' in practice became, 'an unprecedented crusade to raise standards' (Blair, 1999). As in the USA *No Child Left Behind* policy (US Department of Education, no date), educational reform in England has rested on the prescription and assessment of standards of attainment, supported by measures to make teachers accountable for the attainments of their students, and the introduction of market forces to generate competition between schools and so incentivize them to perform at even higher levels.

Where these developments connect with the theme of this book is less in their successes than in their failures. There are two respects in which the reform efforts of recent years have been disappointing. The first is that any improvements in educational standards have failed, by and large, to translate into a closing of the gap between those groups who have traditionally done well in the education system and those who have traditionally done badly. Despite often vigorous efforts at school reform, the education systems of the economically developed world remain characterized by significant levels of inequality (OECD, 2008). Thirteen years after Tony Blair's famous commitment to education, and 21 years after the first major education reform, it was still the case in England that children from poorer backgrounds were likely to do significantly worse than their more advantaged peers, and that educational outcomes were structured also by gender and ethnicity (Schools Analysis and Research Division, 2009). Even more worryingly, this was despite the raft of targeted interventions during the New Labour years to which we referred in chapter one. It is, therefore, difficult to escape the conclusion, as one US scholar of education reform puts it, that much recent thinking is 'flawed by its assumption that schools alone can eliminate achievement gaps in the face of powerful social inequalities in the wider society' (Gamoran, 2007).

Second, a high price has had to be paid for the attempts to reform education systems. The 'crusade for standards' has, in the eyes of many, produced a narrowing of the purposes and practices of schooling (Alexander *et al.*, 2009). The apparatus of tests, central prescription, high-stakes accountability and competition may have raised standards of attainment overall, but it has done so at the expense of the breadth of the curriculum and the extent to which education is able to support the wider personal development of children and young people. When, all those years ago, James Callaghan argued for the need for the education system to produce employable young people, he also claimed that education was a matter of balance between competing aims. 'The balance was wrong in the past', he warned. 'We have a responsibility now to see that we do not get it wrong again in the other direction' (Callaghan, 1976). It seems that his warning has, in some respects at least, been left unheeded.

For some commentators, the narrowing of educational aims and practices is part of a more fundamental shift of political and social values, from what might be called the 'civic' to the 'neo-liberal project' (Gunter *et al.*, 2010, p. 164). The latter emphasizes the role of the state in promoting economic development and in aligning the education system with economic aims. The former, by contrast, emphasizes social justice and participatory democracy, and sees education as a pathway not just to personal development, but to the development of active citizens in a healthy society. The narrowing of the curriculum and focus on measured attainment within the 'crusade for standards', therefore, form part of a much wider reconstruction, not only of what education is for, but of the kind of society for which education is preparing young people. On this analysis, the failure (if it is such) of the standards agenda is both a failure to overturn established patterns of advantage and disadvantage and a failure of democratic society itself.

In the light of this, it seems to us that there are two ways of thinking about what full service and extended school approaches might contribute. One offers a rationale that is broadly consistent with the 'neo-liberal project', but nudges it in the direction of a greater concern for equality and a wider conceptualization of what schools might be and be for. It focuses on how schools might tackle the disadvantages faced by students and their families, and thereby break a link between social background, educational outcomes and life chances that apparently cannot be broken by standards-driven reforms alone. To this extent, it is very much in line with what we have called the dominant rationale for full service and extended schools, but, as we shall see, develops it in some important new directions. The other way of thinking, which has received far less attention, is more closely aligned with the 'civic project'. It focuses on the contribution that full service and extended schools might make to building a vibrant, democratic society. By linking the academic work of schools to the development of their students as active citizens, and by playing a role in the development of the communities they serve, schools might help build a society that is not just economically viable, but is also healthy in terms of its politics and values.

In the following sections, we consider each of these rationales in turn, and explore how they might be elaborated and realized in practice. Our conclusion is that, in reality, the two rationales overlap. In unequal societies, efforts to tackle disadvantage continue to be necessary. However, ultimately, we shall argue, they can only be successful if they are part of a wider attempt to build communities and societies that are based on participatory, democratic principles.

Tackling the problem of disadvantage

National governments, local administrations and head teachers have been faced on the one hand with a powerfully imperative for raising standards of attainment, and on the other with the evidence that large numbers of students cannot learn effectively because of the family and social disadvantages they face. It is scarcely surprising, then, that many have seen full service and extended schools as an answer to their dilemma. Certainly, the proposition that reconfiguring services around schools might solve a range of social and educational problems seems superficially attractive. However, the reality, as we saw in the previous chapter, is that outcomes from attempts to do this are decidedly mixed, and that this relates to the limited capacity of such schools for changing outcomes for communities or disadvantaged groups as a whole.

We suggested earlier that what limits this capacity is the tendency for full service and extended schools to emerge within short-term, school-centred and non-strategic initiatives. As critics of similarly ameliorative initiatives have noted (Power *et al.*, 2005; Rees *et al.*, 2007; Smith, 1987), there is a contradiction between efforts to tackle the local manifestations of disadvantage – the difficulties facing particular individuals in particular communities – and the origins of those difficulties in deeper social structures and inequalities. In effect, these critics argue, such efforts:

> are based on the view that social and economic disadvantage is a 'residual' category, which can therefore be defined in terms of remaining 'pockets' of disadvantage in a wider context of increasing affluence. They do not acknowledge that, in reality, local disadvantage is a particular manifestation of the wider social inequalities which are endemic to societies such as the UK. Far from being an exceptional feature of British society, which can be tackled by special state initiatives . . . areas of social disadvantage are complex, but normal manifestations of the characteristic patterns of social differentiation and inequality in the UK (and elsewhere).
>
> (Rees *et al.*, 2007, p. 271)

Put another way, a smattering of full service and extended schools will change little in societies where social and economic inequalities are rampant, and poverty is allowed to grow.

It is tempting in the light of this critique to conclude that the disadvantage-focused rationale that has dominated thinking about full service and extended schools is fundamentally mistaken. Our view, however, is that it is not so much mistaken as under-developed. It may indeed be naïve to assume that a simple reconfiguration of services around schools will in itself be enough to overcome the effects of structural disadvantage. However, it is equally naïve to assume that social structures produce outcomes in a straightforwardly deterministic way. Both of these views, as we shall see, underestimate the complexity of 'disadvantage' and of the links between structural inequalities and outcomes for individuals. Full service and extended schools, we shall argue, have a role to play in combating disadvantage, but only on the basis of a sophisticated understanding of disadvantage that is neither naïvely optimistic about the possibilities of intervention, nor unduly pessimistic.

Understanding disadvantage

If we are to understand what schools can change in the relationship between social disadvantage and education, we have to understand a little more clearly how that relationship works. As a recent review of the evidence in England argues, there is indeed 'a very clear pathway' from childhood deprivation – understood as adverse family or area economic circumstances – through low educational attainment and on to reduced adult earnings (Schools Analysis and Research Division, 2009, p. 6). There is, moreover, a similar pathway to other adult outcomes – for instance, to poor health, limited life expectancy, and increased criminality (Dyson *et al.*, 2009; Feinstein *et al.*, 2008; Schools Analysis and Research Division, 2009). However, although the pathway may be clear, it is also complex. Economic adversity does not 'produce' poor outcomes in some straightforward way, because children learn and grow in a range of contexts, including family, peer group, neighbourhood and school, amongst others. In each of these contexts, multiple factors are at work, and their impacts and interactions help to shape outcomes. Family characteristics and dynamics, group cultures, community norms, local opportunity structures, and school processes are amongst a wide range of factors that mediate or moderate the effects of economic adversity and lead to children doing more or less well in terms of education and their adult lives (see, for instance, Duckworth, 2008; Irwin *et al.*, 2007; Schoon, 2006).

It is certainly the case that adversity in relation to these factors is associated – often strongly associated – with adversity in economic terms. When, therefore, we use a term such as 'disadvantage', as we have throughout this book, we tend to refer in a shorthand way to this bundle of associated factors. It is also the case that, as advocates of full service and extended schools frequently assert, when these factors are aligned against the prospects of children's doing well, there is relatively little that traditionally organized schools can do to counter the powerful forces at work beyond the school gates (see, for instance, Cassen and Kingdon, 2007; Mortimore and Whitty, 2000). As one American commentator succinctly puts it, 'Our many dedicated teachers can help disadvantaged children significantly. But they can't begin to unravel the complicated and profound problems that children trapped in poverty may bring to the schoolhouse doors' (Neuman, 2009, p. 181).

It follows that ramping up the quality and intensity of instruction, as standards-based reforms in England and elsewhere have sought to do, is unlikely *by itself* to be enough to change the relative achievements of more and less disadvantaged students. This is reason enough for believing that schools need to 'do something' about the adverse factors in many children's lives. However, quite what that 'something' is has to be based on the realization that the relationship between the various contexts in children's lives, and the various factors at work in those contexts, is not necessarily one of simple alignment. Precisely because of the multiplicity of those factors and the complexity of their interactions, it is entirely possible that adversity in one context will be compensated for or ameliorated by positive factors elsewhere. So, for instance, effective family support for learning may be more likely in better-off families, but a child from a poorer family may also receive good support (Desforges and Abouchaar, 2003), or might find the disadvantages from the home background partially ameliorated by attending a particularly supportive and encouraging school (Gorard, 2010).

This means that, whilst adverse economic circumstances increase the likelihood of poor outcomes, this likelihood falls some way short of being a certainty. As Bartley explains:

We know from many studies that people who experience socioeconomic disadvantage have much poorer prospects throughout their life course. It is harder for them to do well at school, to get good, secure, and well paid jobs, and to remain healthy and happy in later life.

There are, however, quite a few people who go through periods of poverty, unemployment, family breakdown and other social disadvantages and yet go on to lead healthy and rewarding lives.

(Bartley, 2006)

Sometimes these likelihoods are conceptualized in terms of the 'risks' that adverse circumstances create, and the 'resilience' in respect of those risks that some people seem to display (Bartley *et al.*, 2007; Schoon, 2006). Resilience in this sense is defined as 'the process of withstanding the negative effects of risk exposure, demonstrating positive adjustment in the face of adversity or trauma, and beating the odds associated with risks' (Bartley, 2006).

As this definition implies, resilience may arise from people's psychological characteristics – their 'positive adjustment', or their capacity to bounce back when things go wrong. However, it may also be ecological, in the sense that it can arise from some other 'protective' factors in their lives, or from the interaction between these factors and individual psychology.

This conceptualization has important implications for the potential role of full service and extended schools. It suggests, for instance, that there is no contradiction between saying on the one hand that such schools cannot tackle the structural causes of disadvantage, and, on the other, that, *at the individual level*, they can have significant impacts on the lives of children and adults. If we regard disadvantage simply as a shorthand term for what is in reality a complex interacting web of factors, we can see how schools can act both to reduce the risks to which individuals are subject, and increase their resilience in the face of those risks. They can, as we have seen, do something about helping parents into work, and helping families through crises, at the same time as they teach children well, develop their independence and confidence, and help them manage their personal difficulties. In itself, this will not change underlying social structures, and the inequalities and adversities inherent in those structures will, therefore, continue to generate risk. However, it may mean that students in a full service or extended school may be a little less likely than those in other schools to encounter those risks, and a little more likely to do well in the face of whatever risks they do encounter.

This in turn has implications for how full service and extended schools might structure their interventions, and for the time-scale over which the effects of their interventions will become apparent. The process of reducing risks and building resilience implies something more than either an opportunistic development of services and activities, or a reactive response to presenting problems. It implies a careful assessment of the risks facing children, families and communities, and of the protective factors that might counter them. It then implies the development of a set of strategic interventions, aimed not so much at dealing with short-term problems, as at increasing the likelihood of positive outcomes at some point in what may well be the distant future.

An example of how this might change the work of schools can be found in the vexed question of how to tackle 'low aspirations'. This has been a recurrent theme in government policy in England, where there has tended to be an assumption of a direct relationship between economic deprivation and a 'poverty of aspiration', which locks individuals, families and whole communities into disadvantage (Blunkett, 2000; DCSF, 2008d). As a result, many of the schools that we have worked with have seen it as a priority for them to 'raise aspirations' amongst their students, usually through a concerted campaign to get them, in the words of one government programme, to 'aim higher' (AIMHIGHER, 2008). It is not perhaps surprising, in the light of the foregoing discussion, to find that this approach turns out to be somewhat simplistic. It is indeed the case that aspirations are important factors in shaping outcomes and life chances, and are strongly impacted upon by economic deprivation (see, for instance Goodman and Gregg, 2010). However, they are neither simply 'produced' by poverty nor straightforwardly malleable in response to exhortation. Young people in disadvantaged circumstances may, in fact, start out with quite high aspirations, but whether they maintain them or, as is often the case, lower them depends on a complex, interacting set of factors. These include their experiences and the way they make sense of those experiences, the material conditions in which they find themselves, and the ways in which they are treated by their schools (Atherton *et al.*, 2009; Sinclair *et al.*, 2010). The formation of 'aspirations', therefore, is a dynamic process, the outcomes of which are neither entirely predetermined nor easily changed.

It follows that simply encouraging people to be more aspirational is likely to have only a limited effect, and, moreover, one that is likely to be dissipated as soon as negative experiences reveal high aspirations to be unrealistic. If full service and extended schools wish to tackle low aspirations, therefore, they have to do so in a much more strategic risk-reducing and resilience-building way. They may need, for instance, to change the nature of opportunities for individuals and opportunity structures in the areas they serve, work to remove material barriers and bring about real successes in people's lives, and work with children, families and communities to explore new ways in which they might understand their worlds. This is likely to demand multiple, undramatic but sustained interventions across a wide range of school, family and community contexts. The effects of such interventions are likely to be indirect, and the final outcomes are likely to become apparent only many years into the future, when people are doing a little better than they otherwise might have done.

As we saw in chapter five, deferred outcomes of this kind pose a challenge in a situation where schools are held accountable for a narrow range of attainment outcomes in the short term. Nonetheless, there is ample evidence that even relatively small-scale interventions at one point in the life course can have important long-term outcomes. We know, for instance, that what schools do can have an impact not just on the short-term health for their students but also, many years down the line, on their longer-term adult health outcomes (Dyson *et al.*, 2009; Hammond and Feinstein, 2006). Similarly, there is the well-known evidence from the High/Scope Perry pre-school study, in which a limited intervention in the early years seems to have had positive lifetime effects on disadvantaged children (Barnett, 1996; Berrueta-Clement *et al.*, 1984; Oden *et al.*, 2000; Schweinhart and Weikart, 1980; Schweinhart *et al.*, 1993; Schweinhart *et al.*, 2005; Weikart *et al.*, 1978). In much the same vein, there is also evidence from England that high-quality pre-school provision has positive effects which last at least until the end of primary school, even if children come from relatively disadvantaged home backgrounds (Sylva *et al.*, 2008). Evidence of this kind, of course, strengthens the case for 'early intervention', understood as intervention early in the life course (see, for instance, Neuman, 2009, p. 181). However, we would argue that intervention in the early years is simply a special case of intervention at an early point in the process whereby the risks facing both children and adults get translated into poor outcomes. It is, we suggest, this kind of intervention with which full service and extended schools should be concerned.

Enhancing full service and extended school approaches

There is a further implication of this more complex understanding of disadvantage. It is to do with what, at various points in this book, we have called the 'scope' of full service and extended school approaches. For the most part, as we have seen, schools seem to have been happiest working with individual students and families, and this certainly is where the strongest evidence of their effectiveness is to be found. Moreover, the focus we have just placed on resilience building might seem to imply that work with individuals is always likely to be most productive. The reality, however, is that a risk-and-resilience approach demands more than a series of individual interventions. It demands, in particular, that the sources of risk are tackled in the wider context of children's lives, and, specifically, in the communities and areas where they live.

Whilst, therefore, schools may not be able to tackle the socio-structural causes of disadvantage, there may be more realistic targets for them and their partners in some of the local conditions – high levels of unemployment, say, or poor educational opportunities, or inadequate transport links, or high levels of street crime – out of which individual disadvantages in part arise. Again, we see no contradiction between an acknowledgement of the underlying structural origins of disadvantage and a wish to address those local conditions through which structural effects are mediated – and through which they may also be moderated. There is, in fact, a long history in England of attempts to address disadvantage at a local level, through what are commonly known as area based initiatives (ABIs). These involve directing additional resources and giving increased flexibilities to disadvantaged areas, whilst encouraging collaboration between agencies to develop a strategic and integrated response (Griggs *et al.*, 2008; Lupton, 2010; Smith, 1999). The results indicate that whilst, as we might expect, ABIs are unlikely to produce large-scale transformations in patterns of disadvantage, they can have some positive, local effects. As Smith puts it 'area targeted programmes are not a panacea and cannot hope to solve everything'. On the other hand:

there is a clear rationale for area targeted interventions. The key reason for this is that some areas suffer disproportionately high levels of economic and social deprivation; including very high levels of worklessness, poverty, poor health, high crime and fear of crime and need special attention. Although some issues can only be addressed through national level mainstream policies it is the case that some problems occur because of local area related factors and it is therefore appropriate to address them at the local level.

(Smith, 1999, p. 49)

We would argue, therefore, that what we currently label as full service and extended school approaches might usefully be reconceptualized as area-based initiatives, to which schools become key contributors. This is not merely a semantic change. There is a considerable difference between, on the one hand, interventions that are marshalled by schools, based on the school site, and driven by school priorities, and, on the other, approaches that involve schools but are formulated at area level, involve a wide range of partners, and pursue priorities that are driven by wider community concerns. This difference can be seen, for instance, in the well-known work of the Harlem Children's Zone in New York. Schools contribute to the work of the Zone, but their work is aligned with that of pre-school programmes, community health initiatives, community organizing, action on housing tenure, and a range of other programmes (Tough, 2008). In this way, the Zone's leaders claim, it is possible to offer not just islands of full-service provision, but:

a unique, holistic approach to rebuilding a community so that its children can stay on track through college and go on to the job market.

The goal is to create a 'tipping point' in the neighborhood so that children are surrounded by an enriching environment of college-oriented peers and supportive adults, a counterweight to 'the street' and a toxic popular culture that glorifies misogyny and anti-social behavior.

(The Harlem Children's Zone, 2009)

Our own work has brought us into close contact with examples in England of similarly wide-ranging and strategically coherent approaches. It is worth examining two of these – Weston Academy and the Bairstow learning centres – to see what we can learn from them about how full service and extended schools might be developed in future.

Example 1: Weston Academy

Academies in the English context are a little like charter schools in the USA, or 'free schools' in Sweden. The academies initiative has evolved continually since its inception. In its first incarnation, however, it opened the way for schools that would be funded by the state, but would remain outside the control of local authorities, and instead would be managed by one or more private or public 'sponsors' (National

Audit Office, 2007). Most of the early academies were established to serve highly disadvantaged areas and replace schools that were judged to have failed to raise attainments in those areas sufficiently. The academies initiative has been hugely controversial in England because it strengthens the role of the private sector in state education and threatens the local democratic control of schools (Curtis *et al.*, 2008). Nonetheless, it has paved the way for new perspectives to be brought to bear on the problems of schooling in disadvantaged areas – perspectives that are not bounded by the assumptions of professional educationalists.

This is certainly the case in Weston Academy, where the sponsor is a local housing trust, whose primary responsibility is the provision of affordable housing for local people. As with many such bodies, the trust sees the provision of housing as being about more than 'bricks and mortar'. Instead, it is concerned with building sustainable communities where people feel safe, get along with each other well, have the skills to compete in the labour market, and so have enough money to enjoy a reasonable quality of life. Already, therefore, the trust employs not only builders, craftspeople and administrators to look after the maintenance and renting of its housing stock, but also community, family and youth workers whose job is to support and enhance the lives of the people who live in its houses. Moreover, it works closely with a wide range of other agencies – including the local authority, the police and the fire service – involved in providing community services.

In this context, the academy offers the trust an important opportunity to enhance what it is already able to do for and with local people. Specifically:

- by developing a high-quality school, the trust is able to enhance the overall attractiveness of the area, reduce the risk of upwardly mobile families moving away to find better schools for their children, and so ensure the diversity of the community;
- by using the school to work directly with children and young people, the trust can enhance the capacity they have to do well for themselves and to contribute to the area; and
- by using the school as a base for services, the trust can offer families and community member's access to the services and opportunities they need, but which might otherwise be difficult for them to access.

In some ways, the academy functions much like many other full service and extended schools. There are, however, some important differences. Within its senior leadership team, for instance, is a community development worker transferred from the trust, and responsible for leading its work with families and communities. The academy's own student and family support workers collaborate closely with the trust's community workers. Children and families in difficulties can be identified by either team, and joint strategies can be developed to address them. The academy has access through the trust to a range of partnerships with other public and voluntary agencies, and to a range of data-sources, that would otherwise remain closed to it. Similarly, as a major employer the trust can offer vocational opportunities to the academy's students that would otherwise be difficult to find. However, it is not principally in these practicalities that the academy is different from other full service and extended schools. It is in the conceptualization of its role. The academy is not simply a school extending the range of its services and activities in order to fulfil better its core educational function. It is, rather, a contributor to a strategy, owned by the trust, for building a sustainable community – within which education may be a key component, but is nonetheless only one element amongst many.

The leaders of the trust admit to having thought long and hard before committing themselves to sponsoring the academy. Such a venture is costly of resources, and carries considerable reputational risks if the academy should find itself in trouble. The commitment, therefore, is based on a detailed analysis of the needs of the area and of what sponsoring an academy might do to meet those needs. As a housing provider with access to a wide range of neighbourhood statistics, to data from partner organizations, and to the experience of its own staff in working with local people, the trust was particularly well-placed to carry out this task. Moreover, as a customer-centred organization, it was used to consulting its tenants and acting on their wishes. It was, therefore, able to feed the views of local people into the analysis in a way that a school might have found more difficult.

Effectively, its analysis took the form of an implicit theory of change of the kind we have encountered throughout this book. The basis of the theory was an understanding of the local area not only as beset by many of the problems characteristic of other disadvantaged areas – low income, poor educational achievements, high levels of crime, poor health and so on – but also as experiencing a particular set of economic circumstances. The area is part of a town with a history of manufacturing based on small- and medium-sized enterprises. There has never been a large employer in the town and, as a result (so the analysis went), local people have become accustomed to accepting low-wage, low-skilled jobs with relatively few opportunities for progression. This situation has been exacerbated by the national shift away from manufacturing towards service- and knowledge-based employment, and by the local manifestation of this in the relocation of opportunities away from the town towards a neighbouring city. Since local people have traditionally expected to find work in their immediate area, these new opportunities are remote both in terms of the skills they demand and the (psychological) distances they require people to travel. As a result, people find themselves somewhat lost in this new world, unable to work their way to a better life and dependent on professionally provided services to solve the problems they encounter.

In this context, the desire to build a sustainable community and to make education central to this task takes on a particular flavour. The development of attitudes and aspirations (in the more complex sense we outlined earlier) is as important as the development of skills. For young people, this means understanding that there are employment opportunities beyond those their parents might have been accustomed to, that these might sometimes lie beyond the town, and that they demand that young people take advantage of the educational opportunities on offer. For all community members, it means developing higher levels of skills, becoming more entrepreneurial, and developing the capacity to solve problems. In this way, the analysis went, the local community will become less dependent, higher skilled and more ambitious, and therefore more attractive to new employers and better able to deal with its own problems.

Example 2: Bairstow and its learning centres

Bairstow Council is responsible for public services – including schools – in a large administrative area on the fringes of a major city. It has carried out an analysis of its situation not unlike that undertaken by the Weston Housing Trust. The decline of manufacturing has hit its neighbouring city harder than most in England, and has created particular problems in Bairstow itself. This is because large parts of the area are made up of housing estates developed to accommodate people moved from 'slum' housing in the city itself. As a result, Bairstow never developed a strong economy of its own, and the restructurings of recent years have seen relatively large numbers of people stranded in worklessness, isolated from job (and many other) opportunities, and mired in the hopelessness of their situation.

The local school system has, the analysis goes, been both the victim of, and a contributor to, this situation. In an area where a traditional indifference to education has been exacerbated by the travails of recent years, attainments are depressingly low and signs of disengagement from education are alarmingly high. At the same time, it has become clear that some schools do a better job than others, and that the primary sector as a whole does much better than the secondary sector. In response, the Council has embarked on a radical reform of its secondary school system, as part of a wider effort to address the social and economic problems of the area. In essence, this involves:

- locating new school buildings so as to serve each of the different localities making up the area for which Bairstow Council is responsible;
- developing a set of pedagogical principles and practices intended to be significantly different from – and substantially more effective than – those which have produced historically low levels of achievement;
- designing the new school buildings in such a way as to facilitate these new pedagogical practices (for instance, by abandoning the traditional structure of enclosed, box-like classrooms);
- expecting all the new schools to offer a range of child and family support, and of community facilities and services, and incorporating accommodation for these into the design of the new buildings;
- linking the new schools to partnerships of service providers, voluntary agencies and community representatives in each locality, so that the work of the schools can be coordinated with wider efforts to develop sustainable communities;
- working towards a unified governance structure for the new schools, so that they work in similar ways towards common aims; and
- locating the development of schooling within the context of an overall strategy for the economic and social development of the Bairstow area.

In many ways, the Bairstow strategy is like the Weston Academy writ large. The new buildings are no longer schools in the traditional sense, and are no longer referred to as such. Instead, they are 'centres for learning' where a number of inter-related activities take place – where children and young people learn, where their families and community members can also learn, where cultural and leisure activities take place, and where child and family services are provided. Moreover, their role is no longer educational in the narrow sense of driving up children's measured attainments, but is oriented much more towards the development of sustainable communities. This certainly involves them in the traditional business of schooling – though the reconstruction of pedagogy and of the spaces where pedagogy happens indicates that even here the traditional boundaries are being pushed. The role of the new centres, however, also embraces the development of sustainable communities and the economic well-being of the area as a whole.

Again, as in the case of Weston Academy, the new centres are able to take on this wider role because of their close relationship with other community services and agencies. In their own right, for instance, they are highly unlikely to be able to attract new employers to the area. However, working with their community partners and within the context of an area economic development strategy, they can help to produce a more skilled workforce with higher expectations, address some of the social problems that have beset the localities they serve, make the area as a whole a better place to live, and so encourage employers to locate their businesses there.

Weston and Bairstow: from hubs to networks and nests

It is important neither to romanticize the Weston and Bairstow developments nor to underestimate their significance. Both initiatives are in their early days. There are encouraging signs that they are beginning to bring about some of the changes they aspire to, but as yet there is no convincing evidence that outcomes – however narrowly or broadly defined – are significantly better than they might have been had less radical approaches been adopted. Our own work, moreover, suggests that there are teething problems, tensions, and possibly quite fundamental flaws in both places (see, for instance, Rowley and Dyson, 2011). It is, for instance, one thing to aspire to change traditional pedagogy or develop a new kind of curriculum, but quite another to enable teachers to make these changes. Likewise, it is one thing to declare that schools will have a broader, community-focused role, but quite another to develop this role at the same time as satisfying the continuing demands of the standards agenda.

On the other hand, something is happening in these cases which takes us not only beyond traditional models of schools, but also beyond established approaches to full service and extended schooling. That 'something', we suggest, is a shift from the *hub* model of full service and extended schools, to a *network* and *nested* model. Schools function as hubs when services and activities are based on their sites and are shaped by their priorities. They function as networks when the focus is not on locating services and activities in the school, but on aligning the work of the school with that of other community agencies, and within the context of a shared local strategy. The limited capacity of the school is then of far less concern, since it is simply one contributor to a network, within which the resources of other agencies and providers are brought to bear in pursuit of a common set of aims.

This in turn has implications for the governance of the school in its extended role. In 'traditional' full service and extended approaches, it tends to be the school and its leaders who decide what services are needed and how they will be provided, albeit very often in consultation with other agencies. In the Weston and Bairstow cases, however, any strategy developed at school level is *nested* within a wider strategy formulated beyond the school – by, in these cases, the housing trust, or the area partnership, or the local authority. This inevitably involves some loss of autonomy by the school. Weston Academy is effectively managed by the housing trust, and the new centres in Bairstow are moving towards a common governance structure, with the consequence that in neither case can schools make unfettered decisions about what they choose to do. However, the benefit of this loss of autonomy is that they are able to work as part of a more powerful and wide-ranging structure. They are no longer restricted to providing a little more curricular or personal support to their students, or some limited family support and a little adult education. Instead they can – as part of the wider structure – seek to impact on some of the underlying factors affecting the communities they serve, for example, on adult skills, on employment, on housing and on street crime.

This more wide-ranging approach has two further implications. First, it both calls for and makes possible a more wide-ranging and coherent analysis than is often found in full service and extended schools. As we have argued throughout this book, developing a theory of change needs to begin with an analysis of the situation in which the school finds itself, and of the problems and possibilities in that situation. So long as interventions are school-driven, however, it is inevitable that they will rely on the perceptions and priorities of school leaders. Sometimes these will be informed by robust data and will take into account the perspectives of other stakeholders. However, we have seen how it is more likely that they will rely on the assumptions and personal knowledge – even prejudices – of school staff. At both Weston Academy and Bairstow, we see a different process at work, because analysis and strategy-formulation take place beyond the school. School leaders may be involved, but the analyses are led by organizations with wider responsibilities for areas and communities, draw on the wide array of information to which these organizations have access, and may involve local people in ways that are not familiar to schools. This is not, of course, a guarantee that the analyses are perfect or free from unwarranted assumptions, but it is striking how in both cases they embrace issues that go well beyond those that schools typically consider.

Second, it is notable in both these cases – but especially in Bairstow – that a genuinely holistic area strategy involves schools in reconstructing their own internal processes and practices. As we indicated in chapter one, there is a history in England of schools seeing the development of a community role as necessitating a fundamental reconsideration of a range of other assumptions about what schools are and are for. We can see this in Morris's vision of Village Colleges as means of 'abolishing the duality of education and ordinary life' (Morris, 1924), and again in the 'radical' community schools of the 1970s (Midwinter, 1973; Watts, 1974). It is arguable that this willingness to look radically at internal school practices has been lost in more recent full service and extended school developments. This may be because the imperatives of standards-based reform, and the preoccupation with removing 'barriers to learning' have marginalized any consideration of what is to be learned and how. Whatever the reason, Weston and Bairstow remind us that a holistic approach cannot afford to overlook how the school sets about its core business of teaching and learning.

The wider context: redefining education policy

The more strategic, area-based approach that we are advocating has implications for the relationship between full service and extended schools and the system-level policy contexts within which they operate. Not surprisingly, given the one-off nature of many such schools, and their tendency (particularly in the USA) to look to non-governmental organizations for support, the issue of policy at the national or sub-national level is rarely discussed in the literature in this field. However, it seems to us that a more complex understanding of disadvantage demands that full service and extended school approaches be set within an appropriate high-level policy context.

There are a number of reasons why this should be the case. Most immediately, if such approaches are to become an established feature of school systems, they need to lose the marginal status which, as we saw in chapter four, has so often bedevilled them in the past. In particular, if, as we argued there, schools are to engage in 'boundary crossing', then the reinforcement of existing boundaries by inappropriate funding and accountability mechanisms, and by a narrowly standards-based conceptualization of their role is not helpful. Put another way, if full service and extended schools are to play an important part in creating more equitable education systems, they can no longer be regarded as optional extras in the school system, embellishing their core business with a few additional services and activities. The implication is that system level policy needs its own theory of change which articulates what these kinds of approaches are and are for.

If, moreover, the work of schools is to be aligned with the work of other local agencies and organizations as we suggest, incentives and structures at a higher policy level need to be put in place to facilitate this alignment. It is no coincidence that the Bairstow and Weston initiatives have emerged at a time of policy development of this kind in England. As we have seen, successive New Labour governments from 1997 onwards placed considerable emphasis on the need for 'joined-up' responses to the multi-dimensional nature of social exclusion. They therefore put in place a range of structures and incentives to encourage collaboration between traditionally separate agencies and services. In particular, Local Strategic Partnerships (HM Government, 2008) brought together all the stakeholders in an area to plan strategically for its development, whilst Children's Trusts (DCSF, 2008b) brought together all those involved in providing services for children and their families. Such structures have by no means been problem-free (see, for instance, National Evaluation of Children's Trust Path-finders, 2007; Russell *et al.*, 2009), and incentives for collaboration have constantly struggled against counter-incentives for school autonomy and for each agency to pursue its own target-driven agenda (Ainscow *et al.*, 2008; Ainscow *et al.*, 2010).

Nonetheless, it is arguable that, by the time of the demise of the New Labour government in 2010, national frameworks had been created within which the potential for collaborative, strategic approaches to emerge at local level was greater than at any time in the recent past. This had the effect of beginning to reconfigure the relationships between schools, local education policy, and other services for children, families and communities. As the subtle shift from an 'extended *schools*' to an 'extended *services*' agenda implies, schools were no longer expected to operate in isolation. Rather, they were seen as part of a network of services operating strategically in pursuit of shared aims. The Weston and, particularly, the Bairstow initiatives, therefore, are simply well-developed examples of a national trend.

Finally, high-level policy is needed also to pull the powerful levers that can tackle disadvantage beyond the area level. As the American scholar of urban education, Jean Anyon, argues:

> Policies such as minimum wage statutes that yield poverty wages, affordable housing and transportation policies that segregate low-income workers of color in urban areas and industrial and other job development in far-flung suburbs where public transport does not reach, all maintain poverty in city neighborhoods and therefore the schools. In order to solve the systemic problems of urban education, then, we need not only school reform but the reform of these public policies. If, as I am suggesting, the macro-economy deeply affects the quality of urban education, then perhaps we should rethink what 'counts' as educational policy. Rules and regulations regarding teaching, curriculum, and assessment certainly count; but, perhaps, policies that maintain high levels of urban poverty and segregation should be part of the educational policy panoply as well. . . .
>
> (Anyon, 2005, pp. 2–3)

The Weston and at Bairstow initiatives show how this rethinking of what counts as education policy might be realized at local level. However, contrary to what some critics (Power *et al.*, 2005; Rees *et al.*, 2007) assert, there is no reason why the development of local strategies to tackle disadvantage should not be set in the context of strategic action of the same kind at national or sub-national level. As we have argued elsewhere (Dyson *et al.*, 2010), different countries, with broadly similar social, political and economic systems do, as a matter of fact, tolerate different levels of disadvantage. Poverty and inequality are not facts of nature, but result to a significant extent from cumulative policy decisions. Whilst it may be difficult to reverse these decisions wholesale in the short term, the evidence is that even marginal changes of direction make some difference. The efforts of recent governments in England, for instance, have, whatever their limitations, had at least some effect on levels of disadvantage

(Hills *et al.*, 2010). At the same time as they developed integrated services, local co-ordinating mechanisms and extended services in and around schools, these governments also introduced a national minimum wage, pursued redistributive fiscal and welfare policies, increased resources for public services (particularly in disadvantaged areas), and introduced equalities legislation. For many critics, this was undoubtedly far too little, and it is certainly the case that the post-1997 developments are fragile at a time of economic uncertainty and under the leadership of a new, more right-wing government. Nonetheless, what was achieved between 1997 and 2010 is enough to demonstrate that local initiatives and progressive policies at the national level are not mutually exclusive alternatives, but can (and, we would argue, should) go hand in hand.

Beyond disadvantage: reshaping the politics of full service and extended schools

So far, we have considered full service and extended school approaches primarily as means of tackling social and educational disadvantage. In so doing, we are in line with the vast majority of thinking in this field. However, it is important we remind ourselves that the association between such approaches and disadvantage is not an invariable one. As we saw in earlier chapters, full service and extended schools can also – as in the case of the Cambridgeshire Village Colleges – be about community sustainability, or – as in the case of SchoolPLUS in Saskatchewan – be about building a particular kind of society.

The problem of focusing exclusively on 'disadvantage' is, as we argued in chapter two, that it almost inevitably creates a particular kind of politics around what schools do. Specifically, it reinforces an asymmetrical relationship between disadvantaged children, families and communities on the one hand, and the professionals who believe they are able to solve the problems created by disadvantage on the other. Professionals, we suggested, tend to retain the power to decide what is in the best interests of local people whilst ascribing to those people a stereotypical identity as 'disadvantaged'. In this way, the people schools ostensibly set out to help may in effect find themselves further marginalized, with their wishes and priorities, their strengths and resources, largely overlooked. We might add that this may particularly be the case where the professionals concerned are school-based educators who, for understandable reasons, see education as the main route out of disadvantage, and evaluate children and families in relation to their capacity to make the most of the opportunities schools have to offer. Despite the undoubted commitment of many educators, therefore, we have found in our own work an overwhelming emphasis on the inadequacies and shortcomings of local people, with much less acknowledgement either of the adversities facing those people, or of their resourcefulness in dealing with those adversities (Crowther *et al.*, 2003; Cummings and Dyson, 2007; Cummings *et al.*, 2010; Cummings *et al.*, 2007a; Cummings *et al.*, 2007b).

These tendencies have negative consequences for children, families and communities over and above the lack of appropriate cultural recognition which they imply. The domination of decision-making by professionals means that poor decisions are likely to be made, because they are not informed by the knowledge and experience of those whom they affect most immediately (Todd, 2007). It also means that efforts to 'help' and 'support' local people are, paradoxically, likely to drive them further into a state of isolation and dependency (Crowson, 2001; Small, 2004). This is a phenomenon that is well-known in the wider field of community development. As Ebersöhn and Eloff explain:

> The dominant approach to development . . . has been needs driven. This approach starts out by focusing on the needs, deficiencies and problems of communities, and accordingly devises strategies to address these needs and problems. [However,] the needs-based approach creates mental maps of communities that encourage its members to think about themselves as fundamentally deficient and as powerless victims of their circumstances.
>
> (Ebersöhn and Eloff, 2006, p. 462)

This deficit-oriented, needs-based approach may be an ever-present danger in work with disadvantaged communities, but it is by no means inevitable. Ebersöhn and Eloff go on to argue for an 'assets-based approach', by which they mean one which focuses 'on the capacities, skills and social resources of people and their communities' (Ebersöhn and Eloff, 2006, p. 462). Lately, such an approach has been deployed in the community health field in England, and the fuller characterization offered there is worth quoting at length:

> The asset approach values the capacity, skills, knowledge, connections and potential in a community. It doesn't only see the problems that need fixing and the gaps that need filling. In an asset approach, the glass is half-full rather than half empty.
>
> The more familiar 'deficit' approach focuses on the problems, needs and deficiencies in a community such as deprivation, illness and health-damaging behaviours. It designs services to fill the gaps and fix the problems. As a result, a community can feel disempowered and dependent; people can become passive recipients of services rather than active agents in their own and their families' lives.
>
> The asset approach is a set of values and principles and a way of thinking about the world. It:
>
> * identifies and makes visible the health-enhancing assets in a community
> * sees citizens and communities as the co-producers of health and well-being, rather than the recipients of services
> * promotes community networks, relationships and friendships that can provide caring, mutual help and empowerment
> * values what works well in an area
> * identifies what has the potential to improve health and well-being

- supports individuals' health and well-being through self-esteem, coping strategies, resilience skills, relationships, friendships, knowledge and personal resources
- empowers communities to control their futures and create tangible resources such as services, funds and buildings.

(Foot and Hopkins, 2010, p. 7)

Characterized in this way, an assets-based approach promises a different kind of politics around work with people experiencing disadvantage. It repositions those people as co-producers of the solutions to their problems, rather than as helpless victims of their circumstances, or dependent beneficiaries of professionals' support. At the same time, it repositions the professionals as facilitators of local people's efforts rather than as sole owners of resources and solutions. In this way, professionals can (and should) reduce their decision-making power, as local people themselves begin to 'control their futures'.

Such an approach sits well with the more complex understanding of disadvantage which we have been advocating. If disadvantage is seen as a monolithic phenomenon which overwhelms its victims and permeates every aspect of their lives, there is little hope that they will be left with assets on which to build, or with the capacity to solve their own problems. However, if, as we have suggested, disadvantage is seen as more complex and multi-dimensional, less deterministic, and with more room for the agency of the people whose lives it affects, then 'being disadvantaged' in no way disqualifies people from co-producing the resources and the solutions they need. The politics around schools and communities can, moreover, be reshaped further where local people are aware of the power at their disposal and are organized in ways which enable them to use it to the full. Examples of this are relatively rare in England – at least, in disadvantaged communities – but in the USA there are traditions of community activism and community organizing which create a vehicle for people to engage with, and bring powerful influence to bear upon, their local schools (Mediratta et al., 2009; Glickman and Scally, 2008; Shirley, 2001; Warren and Hong, 2009). Accordingly, the balance shifts progressively from professionals providing services to a needy community, through professional leadership of developing communities, and onwards to community leadership of schools.

However, this shifting of balances need not imply a simple handing over of power from professionals to communities. As the American scholar of school-community relationships, Mark Warren, points out 'it is not necessary to assume a zero-sum game in which only one side can have power at any one time. Rather relationships should be built on the twin concepts of shared "social capital" and "relational power"' (Warren, 2005, pp. 167–8). In other words, schools should work collaboratively with communities and community agencies, with a view neither to imposing nor relinquishing power, but to increasing the resources they have jointly at their disposal, and enhancing the power they share to get things done. In the context of high levels of disadvantage and rampant inequality, he argues, this is not simply a more respectful way for professionals and communities to work together, but is an essential political move:

[E]xperts and educators acting within the four walls of the school cannot solve the problems of urban schools and inner-city communities, because these problems are the result of fundamentally unequal power relationships in our society. We need an active and engaged citizenry to build the kinds of relationships and the type of power necessary both to transform education school by school *and* to address the broader structures of poverty and racism that trap our youth.

(Warren, 2005, pp. 167–8)

Developments of this kind, of course, are far from unproblematic. This 'new politics' is beset by multiple issues about how communities are defined, how different interests within communities are reconciled, and how the wishes of community members are ascertained, not to mention how local interests sit with a wider national interest. In the English context at least, it raises the added issue about the relationship between direct community engagement with schools, and the long-standing tradition of indirect engagement through democratic bodies – notably, the local authority. Nonetheless, these arguments are, it seems to us, crucial for rethinking full service and extended schools. As Warren acknowledges, such schools are currently in an ambiguous position. They carry a significant risk of disempowering the very communities they seek to serve, yet their deep engagement with those communities means that they also have the potential to work in a participatory and empowering way (Warren, 2005, pp. 167–8). Realizing this potential, we would suggest, requires a conscious attempt by school leaders to reconstruct their relationships with the children, families and adults they serve.

There have been some signs in our work with schools of what such a reconstruction might look like in practice. As we saw in chapter four, some school leaders at the very least acknowledge that there are barriers between them and their communities, even if they struggle to break those barriers down. Moreover, there are also encouraging signs in, for instance, the efforts by Beresford Primary, which we described in chapter three, to support local people in taking control of their own situations, or the work of other schools in encouraging participants to manage extended activities, or, in particular, in the trusting and empowering relationships developed between many individual professionals and the people on whose behalf they worked. Perhaps most encouraging of all is the number of schools we encountered where full service and extended approaches have been understood to require the participation of students in decision-making, and the development of leadership capacity amongst students as future leaders of their communities. These may be small signs, but they indicate that the politics of full service and extended schools are capable of changing, and that the kinds of asymmetrical relationships that have too often characterized such schools in the past are not inevitable.

Beyond disadvantage: reshaping society

There is a further problem with the overwhelming focus on disadvantage in the field of full service and extended schools. It is that it tends to lead to an impoverished view of the kinds of communities – and, ultimately, the kinds of societies – those schools are supposedly helping to build. Where the focus is unremittingly on problems and deficits, what is good and desirable is effectively defined by default. It is simply the absence of those problems and deficits. It is therefore unusual to find anything in the scholarly or policy literature on full service and extended schools which explicitly addresses the question of the 'good life', or the 'vibrant community', or the 'healthy society'. The best we might hope for is the kind of formulation from the Children's Aid Society which we cited in chapter two. 'Community schools', we are told 'are designed to help all students develop into productive adults who are able to earn a decent living, become responsible family members, and contribute to the larger society through good citizenship' (Children's Aid Society, 2001, p. 27).

Whilst these aims are laudable enough, they indicate no searching analysis of what it is that adults might do with their lives beyond 'earning a living', nor what counts as being a 'responsible' family member, nor what 'good citizenship' actually entails. In the absence of such an analysis, assumptions about what is desirable – or, at least, 'normal' – in community and society tend to slip through unchallenged. Even apparently unexceptionable aims such as these carry implications about how society should work and how its members should behave. Given what we have seen of the politics of full service and extended school approaches, it seems likely that such unchallenged assumptions will simply reinforce existing asymmetries of power.

For these reasons, we would argue that any serious rationale should be founded on some more or less explicit formulation of the kind of life full service and extended schools are trying to enable people to lead, and of the kind of community and society they are seeking to build. Whilst this is uncommon in the current situation, it is not unknown. We noted earlier how both the Weston and Bairstow initiatives engaged in some explicit thinking about the kinds of communities they were trying to create. Moreover, the non-disadvantage-focused initiatives we reviewed in chapter two, perhaps not surprisingly, have tended to articulate more fully developed understandings of what, positively, they are trying to create, rather than what, negatively, they are trying to avoid. Henry Morris's (1924) view of Cambridgeshire village life may be redolent of a different place and time, but at least it indicates some notion of what kind of community the Village Colleges were intended to build, and what sorts of lives people might lead within that community. Likewise, the Saskatchewan SchoolPLUS initiative (M Tymchak (chair) Task Force and Public Dialogue on the Role of the School, 2001) has a clear view about the 'new society' based on 'truly human values' that it aims to build.

Basing full service and extended schools on explicit social aims of this kind has significant implications for how the role of those schools in relation to disadvantage is understood. Currently, as we have seen, full service approaches tend to be seen as extraordinary responses to the atypical conditions in disadvantaged communities. They do something different from mainstream schools, in places that are different from those in the mainstream of society. The effect, therefore, is both to marginalize those schools in their education systems and to reinforce the conceptualization of disadvantage as what Rees et al. (2007) call a 'residual' category. However, enabling students to live better lives, and helping to build better communities and societies are – or should be – the concerns of all schools. Full service and extended schools are, therefore, not essentially different in their aims and methods from other schools, but are contributing to a common social and educational mission. Insofar as they have work to do in tackling disadvantage, that work has to be seen as part of the wider task of building a better society, which inevitably – and, we believe, productively – gives rise to the question of what kind of society would make such disadvantage less likely to arise.

Again, there are some small indications of what such a reconceptualization might look like in practice. For all our doubts about where policy in England has been and is going, there are two developments in the New Labour years which seem to us to be particularly helpful in this respect, and to which we referred in chapter one. One is the articulation of the principle of 'progressive universalism', and the other is the associated shift from thinking about extended schools as a separate category to seeing all schools as offering access to extended services. Together, these suggest that all schools are involved in essentially the same endeavour, and that they all need to share, to some extent at least, in the working practices traditionally associated with full service and extended schools. Building better lives, better communities and a better society, the implication is, involves all schools in working holistically with children, and in engaging with their wider family and community contexts. At the same time, the principle of progressive universalism implies that, in an unequal society, it will be necessary for common approaches to be modified in the light of individual and local circumstances, and that some redistribution of resources and efforts may be necessary in order to create greater equality.

Finally, if full service and extended schools are reconceptualized as part of a wider social and educational endeavour, many of the problems around the politics embedded in those schools disappear. The relationship between well-resourced professionals and 'needy' disadvantaged communities may well be inherently asymmetrical. However, the nature of society and of the communities and individual lives sustained by society is the concern of all citizens – and the relationship between school professionals and citizens as a whole does not necessarily privilege the former. Moreover, the specification of what counts as a 'healthy' society necessarily involves a consideration of what count as 'healthy' relationships between citizens, state, and the professionals employed by the state. The Saskatchewan SchoolPLUS example is again helpful here. As we saw in chapter two, the concern with specifying the nature of the 'new society' it seeks to build goes hand in hand with an articulation of how the school should relate to children, families and communities. It is, we suggest, no accident that those relationships are to be based on mutual respect, partnership, respect for cultural diversity, and the active participation of students in decision making.

Towards a rationale for full service and extended schools

Where this chapter – and, indeed, this book – has led us is towards the articulation of a rationale on which the future development of full service and extended schools might be based. Our starting point for that rationale is different from that of most scholars and advocates who have contributed to this field. For us, such schools are not to be seen primarily as responses to the breakdown of communities, to the helplessness of public services in those communities, and to the impossibility of schools' carrying out their core business of teaching children. On the contrary, they are schools like all other schools, helping their students to lead the good life, and helping to build vibrant communities and a healthy society. Everything they do, therefore, should be based on an explicit understanding of – or at least, an open debate about – just what it is that 'good', 'vibrant' and 'healthy' might mean in this context.

With this in mind, we believe there is something to be said for the proposition that all schools should be full service and extended schools, in the sense that they should be working holistically with children, families and communities. However, we also recognize that this will mean different things in different situations. In particular, we accept a principle of progressive universalism which says that, in societies character-ized by inequalities, what is offered to all may need to be enhanced and intensified for those who currently have least. This means that there may be particularly extensive and intensive work to be done in respect of children, families and communities fac-ing what we have referred to throughout this book as 'disadvantage'. We accept the common assumption in this field that working simultaneously within and beyond the school gates offers a means of tackling social disadvantage and its educational impli-cations. Indeed, we would say that there is now enough evidence for us to call this more than an assumption, and to assert that efforts to address educational inequalities by within-school strategies alone are doomed to failure.

We are neither naïvely optimistic, nor unduly pessimistic about what full service and extended schools can achieve. Certainly, they are not, in themselves, a panacea for the social and educational disadvantages that arise in the context of unequal societies. We see them, however, as being capable of making modest improvements in the lives and life chances both of children and adults. We believe that those improvements can be further enhanced if schools see themselves as engaged in a long-term task of reducing the risks to which students, families and communities are subject, and building their resilience to whatever risks remain. We also think they can be enhanced if schools operate not in isolation, but in the context of strategic, area-based approaches. The loss of school autonomy which this involves is, we believe, more than compensated by the added capacity to tackle the local causes of disadvantage which it brings.

We also believe that there are two crucial roles for national policy to play in sup-porting and enhancing the work of these schools. One is to create the context within which full service and extended school approaches can flourish. This means, particu-larly, putting in place appropriately sensitive and sophisticated accountability mea-sures, and facilitating local strategic collaborations. The other is to ensure that school and area strategies for tackling disadvantage are embedded within, and amplified by, equivalent strategies at national and sub-national level. Local responses and progres-sive high-level policies are not mutually exclusive alternatives. Both are needed.

Finally, we believe that, when schools work with children, families and communi-ties, particularly in disadvantaged contexts, they have to be aware of what we have called the 'political' implications of their actions. They have to move away from a model of delivering support to 'needy' people. Instead, they have to work alongside children, families and communities in ways that are characterized by relational power, mutual respect, and the coproduction of solutions to the problems they face. This in turn implies a refocusing from 'needs' to 'assets', and is more likely to happen where the work of schools with disadvantaged individuals and groups is seen as part of the wider task of building better communities and societies.

None of this is easy. In our continuing work in this field, we see plenty of commitment, expertise and goodwill on the part of schools and the professionals working within them. However, we also see this undermined all too often by lack of clear purpose, lack of political sensitivity, and the contradictions of national policy. As we write, the 'remarkable experiment', to which we referred in the first chapter, clings precariously onto life. In a pattern that is all too familiar in the history of full service and extended schools, a government that was committed to their development has been replaced by one that may, if anything, be inclined to see them as little more than an unnecessary interference in the core business of schools (Robson, 2007). If this indeed turns out to be the new policy direction, it will be a great mistake. Schools can ignore what lies beyond their gates, but they cannot escape it. Students bring with them through those gates everything that has happened to them elsewhere in their lives. Families and communities are as present in classrooms as are the students themselves. The choice is not whether to allow the outside world into the school. It is whether to do so openly and thoughtfully, embracing the challenges and opportunities this presents, or to pretend, against all the evidence, that the outside world does not exist. If school leaders and policy makers make the former choice, there may yet come a point where we can agree that full service and extended schools are indeed 'an idea whose time has come'.

References

4ps & Partnership for Schools (2008) *An introduction to Building Schools for the Future,* London: 4ps & Partnership for Schools.

AIMHIGHER (2008) *Aimhigher induction pack.* London: HEFCE & DIUS. Available: www.aimhigher.ac.uk/sites/practitioner/resources/Aimhigher%20induction%20pack%20Sept%2008%20(FINAL).pdf (accessed 13 June 2010).

Ainscow, M., Ayson, A., Goldrick, S., Jones, L. and Kerr, K. (2010) *Equity in education: Creating a fairer education system,* Manchester Centre for Equity in Education, University of Manchester.

Ainscow, M., Dyson, A., Goldrick, S. and Kerr, K. (2008) *Equity in education: Responding to context,* Manchester: Centre for Equity in Education, University of Manchester.

Alexander, R., Armstrong, M., Flutter, J., Hargreaves, L., Harrison, D., Harlen, W., Hartley-Brewer, E., Kershner, R., Macbeath, J., Mayall, B., Northen, S., Pugh, G., Richards, C. and Utting, D. (2009) *Children, their world, their education: Final report and recommendations of the Cambridge Primary Review,* London: Routledge.

Antoniou, L., Dyson, A. and Raffo, C. (2008) 'En Angleterre. Les nouvelles politiques prioritaires (1997–2007), entre incantation et fébrilité', in Demeuse, M., Frandji, D., Greger, D. and Rochex, J.-Y. (Eds) *Évolution des politiques d'éducation prioritaire en Europe: Conceptions, mises en œuvres, débats,* Lyon: INRP.

Anyon, J. (2005) *Radical possibilities: Public policy, urban education and a new social movement,* Abingdon: Routledge.

Argyris, C. and Schön, D. A. (1978) *Organizational learning,* Reading, MA: Addison-Wesley.

Argyris, C. and Schön, D. A. (1996) *Organizational learning II: Theory, method and practice,* Reading, MA: Addison-Wesley.

Atherton, G., Cymbir, E., Roberts, K., Page, L. and Remedios, R. (2009) *How young people formulate their views about the future: Exploratory research.* Research report no. DCSF-RR152, London: DCSF.

Ball, M. (1998) *School inclusion: The school, the family and the community,* York: Joseph Rowntree Foundation.

Ball, S. J. (2008) 'The Legacy of ERA, privatization and the policy ratchet', *Educational Management Administration Leadership,* 36: 185–99.

Barnett, W. S. (1996) *Lives in the balance: Age-27 benefit-cost analysis of the High/Scope Perry preschool program. Monographs of the High/Scope Educational Research Foundation.* Number 11, Ypsilanti, MI: High/Scope Press.

Bartley, M. (2006) *Capability and resilience: Beating the odds.* London: Capability and Resilience Network. Online. Available: www.ucl.ac.uk/capabilityandresilience/beatingtheoddsbook.pdf (accessed 5 June 2010).

Bartley, M., Schoon, I., Mitchell, R. and Blane, D. (2007) *Resilience as an asset for healthy development.* Online. Available: www.ucl.ac.uk/capabilityandresilience/resilienceasanassetforhealthydevelopment.doc (accessed 10 March 2009).

Bash, L. and Coulby, D. (1989) *The Education Reform Act: Competition and control,* London: Cassell.

Belsky, J., Barnes, J. and Melhuish, E. (Eds) (2007) *The national evaluation of Sure Start: Does area-based early intervention work?,* Bristol: The Policy Press.

Benn, C. and Simon, B. (1972) *Half way there: Report on the British comprehensive school reform,* Harmondsworth: Penguin Books.

Bernstein, B. (1970) 'Education cannot compensate for society', *New Society,* 344–7.

Berrueta-Clement, J., Schweinhart, L. and Barnett, W. (1984) *Changed lives: The effects of the Perry Preschool program on youths through age 19. Monographs of the High/Scope Educational Research Foundation.* Number 8, Ypsilanti, MI: High/Scope Press.

Beveridge, S. W. (1942) *Social insurance and allied services,* London: HMSO.

Big Lottery Fund (2006) *Programmes for young people: What we have learned.* London: Big Lottery Fund.

Blair, T. (1996) *The twentieth anniversary lecture given by the Rt Hon Tony Blair 16 December 1996.* London: The Guardian. Online. Available: http://education.guardian.co.uk/thegreatdebate/story/0,,586338,00.html (accessed 7 May 2008).

Blair, T. (1999) *Speech by the Prime Minister Tony Blair about Education Action Zones – 15 January 1999.* London: 10 Downing Street. Online. Available: www.number-10.gov.uk/output/Page1172.asp (accessed 24 May 2004).

Blair, T. (2005) *Education and regeneration.* 18 November 2005. London: 10 Downing Street.

Blank, M., Mclaville, A. and Shah, B. (2003) *Making the difference: Research and practice in community schools,* Washington DC: Coalition for Community Schools, Institute for Educational Leadership. Online. Available: www.communityschools.org/mtdhomepage.html (accessed 2 April 2007).

Blunkett, D. (1999) *Excellence for the many, not just the few: Raising standards and extending opportunities in our schools. The CBI President's Reception Address by the Rt. Hon. David Blunkett MP 19 July 1999,* London: DfEE.

Blunkett, D. (2000) *Raising aspirations for the 21st Century. Speech to the North of England Education Conference, Wigan, 6 January 2000,* London: DfEE.

Brookes, M. (2006) *Taking control. Speech by Mick Brookes, General Secretary NAHT, to Annual Conference on Monday 1 May 2006 at 11.30am.* Haywards Heath: NAHT. Online. Available: www.naht.org.uk/newsdocs/814/conferencespeech2006-mickbrookes.doc (accessed 1 September 2006).

Callaghan, J. (1976) *Towards a national debate (The full text of the speech by Prime Minister James Callaghan, at a foundation stone-laying ceremony at Ruskin College, Oxford, on October 18 1976).* London: The Guardian. Online. Available: http://education.guardian.co.uk/print/0,3858,4277858-109002,00.html (accessed 24 December 2001).

Cameron, C., Moss, P., Owen, C., Petrie, P., Potts, P., Simon, A. and Wigfall, V. (2009) 'Working together in extended schools and children's centres: A study of inter-professional activity in England and Sweden', *Research Brief DCSF-RBX-09–10,* London: DCSF.

Cassen, R. and Kingdon, G. (2007) *Tackling low educational achievement,* York: Joseph Rowntree Foundation.

Central Advisory Council for Education (England) (1967) *Children and their primary schools. Volume 1: Report,* London: HMSO.

Chamberlain, T., Rutt, S. and Fletcher-Campbell, F. (2006) *Admissions: Who goes where? Messages from the statistics*, Slough: NFER.

Chapman, C. and Gunter, H. (2009) 'A decade of New Labour reform of education', in Chapman, C. and Gunter, H. (Eds) *Radical reforms: Perspectives on an era of educational change*, London: Routledge.

Children's Aid Society (2001) *Building a community school*, New York: Children's Aid Society.

Clark, H. and Grimaldi, C. (2005) 'Evaluation of Children's Aid Society community schools', in Dryfoos, J. G., Quinn, J. and Barkin, C. (Eds) *Community schools in action: Lessons from a decade of practice*, Oxford: Oxford University Press.

Clark, J., Dyson, A. and Millward, A. (1999) *Housing and schooling: A case-study in joined-up problems*, York: YPS.

Coalition for Community Schools (2009) *Community schools research brief 09*, Washington DC: Coalition for Community Schools.

Coalition for Community Schools (no date-a) *Community schools: Partnerships for excellence*, Washington DC: Coalition for Community Schools. Online. Available: www.communityschools.org/assets/1/Page/partnershipsforexcellence.pdf#xml=http://pr-dtsearch001.americaneagle.com/service/search.asp?cmd=pdfhits&DocId=68&Index=F%3a%5cdtSearch%5ccommunityschools&HitCount=23&hits=47+48+49+81+a5+c2+e3+e4+11e+11f+120+4b5+4e4+778+e61+1217+12c4+1364+1623+16c9+1906+1a51+1ae2+&hc=3683&req=partnerships+for+excellence (accessed 16 July 2010).

Coalition for Community Schools (no date-b) *Frequently asked questions about community schools*, Washington DC: Coalition for Community Schools. Online. Available: www.communityschools.org/aboutschools/faqs.aspx (accessed 16 July 2010).

Comer, J. P. and Emmons, C. (2006) 'The research program of the Yale Child Study Center school development program', *The Journal of Negro Education*, 75: 353–72.

Committee on Child Health Services (SDM Court chair) (1976) *Fit for the future (The Court Report)*. Volume 1, Cmnd 6684; Volume 2, Cmnd 6684. London: HMSO.

Connell, J. and Klem, A. M. (2000) 'You can get there from here: Using a theory of change approach to plan urban education reform', *Journal of Educational and Psychological Consulting*, 11: 93–120.

Connell, J. P. and Kubisch, A. C. (1998) 'Applying a theory of change approach to the evaluation of comprehensive community initiatives: Progress, prospects and problems', in Fulbright-Anderson, K., Kubisch, A. C. and Connell, J. P. (Eds) *New Approaches to Evaluating Community Initiatives. Volume 2: Theory, measurement and analysis*, Queenstown: The Aspen Institute.

Cox, C. B. and Dyson, A. E. (Eds) (1971) *The Black Papers on education (1969, 1970)*, London: Davis-Poynter.

Crowson, R. L. (2001) 'Community development and school reform: An overview', in Crowson, R. L. (Ed.) *Community Development and School Reform*, London: JAI.

Crowther, D., Cummings, C., Dyson, A. and Millward, A. (2003) *Schools and area regeneration*, Bristol: The Policy Press.

Cummings, C. and Dyson, A. (2007) 'The role of schools in area regeneration', *Research Papers in Education*, 22: 1–22.

Cummings, C., Dyson, A., Jones, L., Laing, K., Scott, K. and Todd, L. (2010) *Evaluation of extended services: Thematic review: Reaching disadvantaged groups and individuals*, London: DCSF.

Cummings, C., Dyson, A., Muijs, D., Papps, I., Pearson, D., Raffo, C., Tiplady, L., Todd, L. and Crowther, D. (2007a) *Evaluation of the Full Service Extended Schools Initiative: Final report. Research report RR852*, London: DfES.

Cummings, C., Dyson, A., Papps, I., Pearson, D., Raffo, C., Tiplady, L. and Todd, L. (2006) *Evaluation of the Full Service Extended Schools Initiative, Second Year: Thematic papers*, London: DfES.

Cummings, C., Dyson, A., Papps, I., Pearson, D., Raffo, C. and Todd, L. (2005) *Evaluation of the Full Service Extended Schools Initiative: End of first year report*, London: DfES.

Cummings, C., Dyson, A. and Todd, L. (2007b) 'Towards extended schools? How education and other professionals understand community-oriented schooling', *Children & Society*, 21: 189–200.

Cummings, C., Dyson, A., Todd, L. with the Education Policy and Evaluation Unit University of Brighton (2004) *An evaluation of the extended schools pathfinder projects. Research report 530*, London: DfES.

Curtis, A., Exley, S., Sasia, A., Tough, S. and Whitty, G. (2008) *The Academies programme: Progress, problems and possibilities*, London: The Sutton Trust.

Davies, R. (2005) 'Scale, complexity and the representation of theories of change part II', *Evaluation*, 11: 133–49.

Davies, R. J. (2004) 'Scale, complexity and the representation of theories of change', *Evaluation*, 10: 101–21.

DCSF (2007) *Guidance on the duty to promote community cohesion*, London: DCSF.

DCSF (2008a) *21st century schools: A world class education for every child*, London: DCSF.

DCSF (2008b) *Children's Trusts: Statutory guidance on inter-agency cooperation to improve well-being of children, young people and their families*, London: DCSF.

DCSF (2008c) *National Healthy Schools Programme*. Online. Available: www.teachernet.gov.uk/wholeschool/healthyliving/nhsp/ (accessed 2 March 2009).

DCSF (2008d) *The extra mile: How schools succeed in raising aspirations in deprived communities*. London, DCSF. Online. Available: www.publications.teachernet.gov.uk/eOrderingDownload/3882_The%20Extra%20Mile_web.pdf (accessed 13 June 2010).

Dean, C., Dyson, A., Gallannaugh, F., Howes, A. and Raffo, C. (2007) *Schools, governors and disadvantage*, York: Joseph Rowntree Foundation.

Department of Education. Directorate: Inclusive Education (Republic of South Africa) (2005) *Conceptual and operational guidelines for the implementation of inclusive education: Full-service schools*, Pretoria: Department of Education.

Desforges, C. and Abouchaar, A. (2003) *The impact of parental involvement, parental support and family education on pupil achievement and adjustment: A literature review. Research report 433*, London: DfES.

DfEE (1999) *Schools Plus: Building learning communities. Improving the educational chances of children and young people from disadvantaged areas: A report from the Schools Plus Policy Action Team 11*, London: DfEE.

DfEE and DSS (1998) *Meeting the childcare challenge: A framework and consultation document. Cm3959*, London: DfEE & DSS.

DfES (2002a) *Childcare in extended schools: Providing opportunities and services for all*, London: DfES.

DfES (2002b) *Time for standards, volume 2010*, London: DfES Publications.

DfES (2003a) *Every Child Matters. Cm. 5860*, London: The Stationery Office.

DfES (2003b) *Full Service Extended Schools: Requirements and specifications*, London: DfES.

DfES (2003c) *Full-Service Extended Schools planning documents*, London: DfES.

DfES (2005a) *Aiming High: Partnerships between schools and traveller education support services in raising the achievement of Gypsy Traveller pupils*, London: DfES. Online. Available: http://nationalstrategies.standards.dcsf.gov.uk/node/84919 (accessed 16 July 2010).

DfES (2005b) *Extended schools: Access to opportunities and services for all. A prospectus*, London: DfES.

Dobbs, J. (2001) *Community schools: Planning space for democracy and civic engagement.* Tennessee Consortium for the Development of Full-Service Schools. Online. Available: http://web. utk.edu/~fss/ (accessed 5 January 2010).

Dryfoos, J. (1994) *Full-Service Schools,* San Francisco: Jossey-Bass.

Dryfoos, J. and Quinn, J. (2005) 'Issue editors' notes', *New directions for youth development,* 2005: 5–6.

Dryfoos, J. G. (2000) *Evaluation of community schools: Findings to date,* Washington DC: Coalition for Community Schools.

Dryfoos, J. G. (2005) 'Preface', in Dryfoos, J. G., Quinn, J. and Barkin, C. (Eds) *Community schools in action: Lessons from a decade of practice,* Oxford: Oxford University Press.

Duckworth, K. (2008) *The influence of context on attainment in primary school: Interactions between children, family and school contexts,* London: Centre for Research on the Wider Benefits of Learning, Institute of Education.

Dyson, A., Gunter, H., Hall, D., Raffo, C., Jones, L. and Kalambouka, A. (2010) 'What is to be done? Implications for policy makers', in Raffo, C., Dyson, A., Gunter, H., Hall, D., Jones, L. and Kalambouka, A. (Eds) *Education and poverty in affluent countries,* London: Routledge.

Dyson, A., Hertzman, C., Roberts, H., Tunstill, J. and Vaghri, Z. (2009) *Childhood development, education and health inequalities. Task group report to the Strategic Review of Health Inequalities in England Post 2010 (Marmot Review),* London: University College London.

Dyson, A., Millward, A. and Todd, L. (2002) *A study of the extended schools demonstration projects. Research report 381,* London: DfES.

Dyson, A. and Todd, L. (2010) 'Dealing with complexity: Theory of change evaluation and the Full Service Extended Schools Initiative', *International Journal of Research and Method in Education,* 33: 119–34.

Ebersöhn, L. and Eloff, I. (2006) 'Identifying asset-based trends in sustainable programmes which support vulnerable children', *South African Journal of Education,* 26: 457–72.

Edwards, A., Barnes, M., Plewis, I., Morris, K. *et al.* (2006) *Working to prevent the social exclusion of children and young people: Final lessons from the National Evaluation of the Children's Fund. Research report No. 374,* London: DfES.

Edwards, A., Daniels, H., Gallagher, T., Leadbetter, J. and Warmington, P. (2009) *Improving interprofessional collaborations: Learning to do multi-agency work,* London: Routledge.

Edwards, A., Lunt, I. and Stamou, E. (2010) 'Inter-professional work and expertise: New roles at the boundaries of schools', *British Educational Research Journal,* 36: 27–45.

Eisenhower Foundation (2005) *Full-Service community schools replication handbook.* Online. Available: www.eisenhowerfoundation.org/docs/FSCS_Handbook_2005.pdf (accessed 6 January 2010).

Feinstein, L., Budge, D., Vorhaus, J. and Duckworth, K. (2008) *The social and personal benefits of learning: A summary of key research findings,* London: Centre for Research on the Wider Benefits of Learning, Institute of Education.

Finkelstein, N. D. and Grubb, W. N. (2000) 'Making sense of education and training markets: Lessons from England', *American Educational Research Journal,* 37: 601–31.

Foot, J. and Hopkins, T. (2010) *A glass half-full: How an asset approach can improve community health and well-being,* London: IDeA.

Full-service Schools Roundtable *Rationale.* Full-service schools roundtable: Boston, MA. Online. Available: www.fssroundtable.org/rationale.htm (accessed 6 January 2010).

Gamoran, A. (2007) 'Introduction: Can standards-based reform help reduce the poverty gap in education?', in Gamoran, A. (Ed.) *Standards-based reform and the poverty gap: Lessons for 'No Child Left Behind',* Washington DC: Brookings Institution Press.

Glaser, B. and Strauss, A. (1967) *The discovery of grounded theory,* Chicago: Aldine.

Glickman, N. J. and Scally, C. P. (2008) 'Can community and education organizing improve inner-city schools?', *Journal of Urban Affairs,* 30: 557–77.

Goodman, A. and Gregg, P. (Eds) (2010) *Poorer children's educational attainment: How important are attitudes and behaviour?,* York: Joseph Rowntree Foundation.

Gorard, S. (2010) 'Education can compensate for society – a bit', *British Journal of Educational Studies,* 58.

Government of Saskatchewan (no date) *SchoolPLUS at a glance.* Regina: Government of Saskatchewan. Online. Available: www.education.gov.sk.ca/adx/aspx/adxGetMedia.aspx?DocID=283,589,144,107,81,1,Documents&MediaID=2073&Filename=ataglance.pdf (accessed 8 January 2010).

Griggs, J., Whitworth, A., Walker, R., McLennan, D. and Noble, M. (2008) *Person- or place-based policies to tackle disadvantage? Not knowing what works,* York: Joseph Rowntree Foundation.

Gunter, H., Raffo, C., Hall, D., Dyson, A., Jones, L. and Kalambouka, A. (2010) 'Policy and the policy process', in Raffo, C., Dyson, A., Gunter, H., Hall, D., Jones, L. and Kalambouka, A. (Eds) *Education and poverty in affluent countries,* London: Routledge.

Halsey, K., Gulliver, C., Johnson, A., Martin, K. and Kinder, K. (2005) *Evaluation of Behaviour and Education Support Teams. Research report RR706,* London: DfES.

Hammond, C. and Feinstein, L. (2006) *Are those who flourished at school healthier adults? What role for adult education? Wider Benefits of Learning Research Reports.* London: Centre for Research on the Wider Benefits of Learning, Institute of Education.

Hattie, J. (2009) *Visible learning: A synthesis of over 800 meta-analyses relating to achievement,* Abingdon: Routledge.

Henderson, A. T. and Mapp, K. L. (2002) *A new wave of evidence: The impact of school, family, and community connections on student achievement: Annual synthesis 2002,* Austin, TX: Southwest Educational Development Laboratory.

Hills, J. C., Brewer, M., Jenkins, S., Lister, R., Lupton, R., Machin, S., Mills, C., Modood, T., Rees, T. and Riddell, S. (2010) *An anatomy of economic inequality in the UK: Report of the National Equality Panel,* London: Government Qualities Office and Centre for Analysis of Social Exclusion.

HM Government (2007) *Extended schools: Building on experience,* London: DCSF.

HM Government (2008) *Creating strong, safe and prosperous communities: Statutory guidance, Department of Communities and Local Government,* London: Communities and Local Government Publications.

Humphrey, N., Kalambouka, A., Bolton, J., Lendrum, A., Wigelsworth, M., Lennie, C. and Farrell, P. (2008) *Primary Social and Emotional Aspects of Learning (SEAL): Evaluation of small group work. Research report No. DCSF-RR064,* London: DCSF.

Irwin, L. G., Siddiqi, A., Hertzman, C. and The Early Child Development Network (2007) *Early child development: A powerful equalizer, final report of the Early Child Development Knowledge Network of the Commission on Social Determinants of Health,* Geneva: World Health Organization.

James-Burdumy, S., Dynarski, M., Moore, M., Deke, J., Mansfield, W. and Pistorino, C. (2005) *When schools stay open late: The national evaluation of the 21st Century Community Learning Centers Program. Final report: U.S. Department of Education.* Institute of Education Sciences, National Center for Education Evaluation and Regional Assistance. Online. Available: www.mathematica-mpr.com/publications/pdfs/21stfinal.pdf (accessed 27 April 2010).

Jeffs, T. (1999) *Henry Morris. Village colleges, community education and the ideal order,* Ticknall: Educational Heretics Press.

Kelly, R. (2005) *Education and social progress. 26 July 2005,* London: DfES. Online. Available: www.dfes.gov.uk/speeches/speech.cfm?SpeechID=242 (accessed 2 August 2005).

Kendall, L., O'Donnell, L., Golden, S., Ridley, K., Machin, S., Rutt, S., McNally, S., Schagen, I., Meghir, C., Stoney, S., Morris, M., West, A. and Noden, P. (2005) *Excellence in cities: The National Evaluation of a policy to raise standards in urban schools 2000–2003. Research report RR675A*, London: DfES.

Kerosuo, H. and Engestrom, Y. (2003) 'Boundary crossing and learning in creation of new work practice', *Journal of Workplace Learning*, 15: 345–51.

Keyes, M. C. and Gregg, S. (2001) *School-community connections: A literature review*, Charleston, WV: AEL, Inc.

Leitch, L. (2006) *The Leitch review of skills: Prosperity for all in the global economy – world class skills. Final report*, London: The Stationery Office.

Lupton, R. (2010) 'Area-based initiatives in English education: What place for place and space?', in Raffo, C., Dyson, A., Gunter, H., Hall, D., Jones, L. and Kalambouka, A. (Eds) *Education and poverty in affluent countries*, London: Routledge.

Lyons, M. (2006) *National prosperity, local choice and civic engagement: A new partnership between central and local government for the 21st century, Lyons Inquiry into Local Government*, London: HMSO.

M Tymchak (chair) Task Force and Public Dialogue on the Role of the School (2001) *SchoolPLUS: A vision for children and youth. Toward a new school, community and human service partnership in Saskatchewan. Final Report to the Minister of Education, Government of Saskatchewan*, Saskatchewan: Government of Saskatchewan.

Mackenzie, M. and Blamey, A. (2005) 'The practice and the theory: Lessons from the application of a theories of change approach', *Evaluation*, 11: 151–68.

Maxwell, J. A. (2004) 'Causal explanation, qualitative research, and scientific inquiry in education', *Educational Researcher*, 33: 3–11.

Mediratta, K., Shah, S. and McAlister, S. (2009) *Community organizing for stronger schools: Strategies and successes*, Cambridge, MA: Harvard Education Press.

Midwinter, E. (1973) *Patterns of community education*, London: Ward Lock.

Moon, B. (Ed.) (1983) *Comprehensive schools: Challenge and change*, London: NFER/Nelson.

Morris, H. (1924) *The Village College. Being a memorandum on the provision of educational and social facilities for the countryside, with special reference to Cambridgeshire*. infed (originally, University Press, Cambridge): London. Online. Available: www.infed.org.uk/archives/e-texts/morris-m.htm (accessed 2 May 2005).

Mortimore, P. and Whitty, G. (2000) 'Can school improvement overcome the effects of educational disadvantage?', in Cox, T. (Ed.) *Combating educational disadvantage: Meeting the needs of vulnerable children*, London: Falmer Press.

National Audit Office (2007) *The Academies programme*, London: The Stationery Office.

National Evaluation of Children's Trust Pathfinders (2007) *National Evaluation of Children's Trust Pathfinders final report*, London: University of East Anglia in association with the National Children's Bureau, for the Department for Education and Skills and the Department of Health. Online. Available: www.dcsf.gov.uk/everychildmatters/resources-and-practice/IG00209/ (accessed 16 July 2010).

National Evaluation of Sure Start (2005) *National evaluation report: Early impacts of Sure Start local programmes on children and families. Research report NESS/2005/FR/013*, London: DfES.

National Strategy for Neighbourhood Renewal (2000) *Report of Policy Action Team 17: Joining it up locally*, London: Department of the Environment, Transport and the Regions.

Neuman, S. B. (2009) *Changing the odds for children at risk: Seven essential principles of educational programs that break the cycle of poverty*, London: Teachers College Press.

Oden, S., Schweinhart, L. J. and Weikart, D. P. (2000) *Into adulthood: A study of the effects of Head Start*, Ypsilanti, MI: High/Scope Press.

OECD (2008) *Ten steps to equity in education*, Paris: OECD Publishing.

OECD (no date) *PISA – the OECD programme for international student assessment*. Paris, OECD. Online. Available: www.oecd.org/dataoecd/51/27/37474503.pdf (accessed 3 June 2010).

Ofsted (2005) *Extended schools: A report on early developments. HMI 2453*, London: Ofsted.

Phillips, R. and Harper-Jones, G. (2003) 'Whatever next? Education policy and New Labour: The first four years, 1997–2001', *British Educational Research Journal*, 29: 125–32.

Power, S., Rees, G. and Taylor, C. (2005) 'New Labour and educational disadvantage: The limits of area-based initiatives', *London Review of Education*, 3: 101–16.

Prescott, J. (2002) *Mainstreaming social justice for the 21st Century*, speech delivered to the Fabian Society/New Policy Institute conference, 'Building Partnerships for Social Inclusion' – Congress House, Great Russell Street. London: Cabinet Office. Online. Available: www. archive.cabinetoffice.gov.uk/ministers/ministers/2002/dpm/fabian%2015%2001% 2002v2.htm (accessed 17 December 2009).

Raffo, C., Dyson, A., Gunter, H., Hall, D., Jones, L. and Kalambouka, A. (2007) *Education and poverty: A critical review of theory, policy and practice*, York: Joseph Rowntree Foundation.

Rees, G., Power, S. and Taylor, C. (2007) 'The governance of educational inequalities: The limits of area-based initiatives', *Journal of Comparative Policy Analysis*, 9: 261–74.

Renewal Trust (no date) *How to define the problem*. Online. Available: www.renewal.net/ Documents/RNET/Overview/How%20To/Howdefineproblem.DOC (accessed 12 April 2007).

Richardson, J. W. (2009) *The full-service community schools movement: Lessons from the James Adams Community School*, Basingstoke: Palgrave Macmillan.

Riddell, S. and Tett, L. (2004) 'New Community Schools and inter-agency working: Assessing the effectiveness of social justice initiatives', *London Review of Education*, 2: 219–28.

Robson, R. C. (2007) *Breakthrough Britain: Ending the costs of social breakdown. Volume 3: Educational failure*, London: The Centre for Social Justice.

Rowley, H. and Dyson, A. (2011) 'Academies in the public interest – a contradiction in terms?', in Gunter, H. M. (Ed.) *The state and education policy: The academies programme*, London: Continuum.

Russell, H., Johnston, L. and Jones, D. (2009) *Long term evaluation of local area agreements and local strategic partnerships Report on the 2008 survey of all English local strategic partnerships. Volume 1 – Executive summary and survey report*, London: Department for Communities and Local Government.

Ryan, G. (2004) *Get it right first time: An education strategy for Ballymun*, Dublin: Ballymun Partnership.

Sallis, J. (2000) *Basics for school governors*, Stafford: Network Educational Press Ltd.

Salm, T. (2007) *Interprofessional partnerships: The challenge and possibility for social justice in (the) light of SchoolPLUS. Research report #07–04*. Saskatchewan School Boards Association: Regina, Saskatchewan. Online. Available: www.saskschoolboards.ca/old/ ResearchAndDevelopment/ResearchReports/StudentsDiverseNeeds/07-04.pdf (accessed 8 January 2010).

Salm, T. L. (2009) *How human service providers can collaborate to improve education: a case study of the Saskatchewan SchoolPLUS project*, Lewiston, NY: Edwin Mellen Press.

Sammons, P., Power, S., Elliot, K., Robertson, P., Campbell, C. and Whitty, G. (2003) *New Community Schools in Scotland. Final report. National evaluation of the pilot phase*, London: Institute of Education, University of London.

Schools Analysis and Research Division Department for Children Schools and Families (2009) *Deprivation and education: The evidence on pupils in England, Foundation Stage to Key Stage 4*, London: DCSF.

Schoon, I. (2006) *Risk and resilience: Adaptations in changing times*, Cambridge: Cambridge University Press.

Schweinhart, L., Barnes, H. and Weikart, D. (1993) *Significant benefits: The High/Scope Perry preschool study through age 27*, Ypsilanti, MI: High/Scope Educational Research Foundation.

Schweinhart, L. and Weikart, D. (1980) *Young children grow up: The Effects of the Perry preschool program on youths through age 15. Monographs of the High/Scope Educational Research Foundation. Number 7*, Ypsilanti, MI: High/Scope Educational Research Foundation.

Schweinhart, L. J., Montie, J., Xiang, Z., Barnett, W. S., Belfield, C. R. and Nores, M. (2005) *Lifetime effects: The High/Scope Perry preschool study through age 40. (Monographs of the High/Scope Educational Research Foundation, 14)*, Ypsilanti, MI: High/Scope Press.

Shaw, C., Harnett, R., Harker, R., Franklin, A. and Olle, H. (2003) *'Becoming Seamless'. An evaluation of Schools Plus Teams pilot project*, London: DfES.

Shemilt, I., O'Brien, M., Thoburn, J., Harvey, I., Belderson, P., Robinson, J. and Camina, M. (2003) 'School breakfast clubs, children and family support', *Children and Society*, 17: 100–12.

Shirley, D. (2001) 'Linking community organizing and school reform: A comparative analysis', in Crowson, R. L. (Ed.) *Community Development and School Reform*, Oxford: JAI.

Sinclair, S., McKendrick, J. H. and Scott, G. (2010) 'Failing young people? Education and aspirations in a deprived community', *Education, Citizenship and Social Justice*, 5: 5–20.

Small, M. L. (2004) *Villa Victoria: The transformation of social capital in a Boston barrio*, London: University of Chicago Press.

Smith, G. (1987) 'Whatever happened to Educational Priority Areas?', *Oxford Review of Education*, 13: 23–38.

Smith, G. R. (1999) *Area-based initiatives: The rationale and options for area targeting. CASE paper 25*, London: Centre for Analysis of Social Exclusion, London School of Economics.

Social Exclusion Task Force (2009) Context for social exclusion work. London: Cabinet Office Social Exclusion Task Force.

Social Exclusion Unit (1998) *Bringing Britain together: A National Strategy for Neighbourhood Renewal, Cm. 4045*, London: The Stationery Office.

Social Exclusion Unit (2000) *National Strategy for Neighbourhood Renewal: A framework for consultation*, London: The Stationery Office.

Social Exclusion Unit (2001) *A new commitment to Neighbourhood Renewal: National Strategy Action Plan*, London: Social Exclusion Unit.

Stame, N. (2004) 'Theory-based evaluation and types of complexity', *Evaluation*, 10: 58–76.

Sylva, K., Melhuish, E., Sammons, P., Siraj-Blatchford, I. and Taggart, B. (2008) *Final report from the primary phase: Pre-school, school and family influences on children's development during Key Stage 2 (Age 7–11)*, London: DCSF.

Szirom, T., Jaffe, R., MacKenzie, D. and Strategic Partners in association with the Centre for Youth Affairs and Development (2001) *National evaluation report. Full service schools program 1999 and 2000*, Canberra: Commonwealth Department of Education, Training and Youth Affairs. Online. Available: www.dest.gov.au/archive/schools/publications/2001/fss/evaluation.pdf (accessed 16 July 2010).

The Dutch Community School Steering Group (2004) *The community school 0–12 years*, Utrecht, Netherlands.

The Harlem Children's Zone (2009) *The HCZ project: 100 blocks, one bright future*. New York, The Harlem Children's Zone. Online. Available: www.hcz.org/about-us/the-hcz-project (accessed 7 March 2010).

The National Evaluation of Sure Start Research Team (2008) *The impact of Sure Start local programmes on three year olds and their families, Report 027*, London: DCSF/HMSO.

The Scottish Office (1998) *New community schools: The prospectus,* Edinburgh: The Stationery Office.

Todd, L. (2007) *Partnerships for inclusive education: A critical approach to collaborative working,* London: Routledge.

Tough, P. (2008) *Whatever it takes: Geoffrey Canada's quest to change Harlem and America,* Boston: Houghton Mifflin Co.

Tsui, A. B. M. and Law, D. Y. K. (2007) 'Learning as boundary-crossing in school-university partnership', *Teaching and Teacher Education: An International Journal of Research and Studies,* 23: 1289–1301.

Tuomi-Grohn, T. and Engestrom, Y. (2007) *Between school and work: New perspectives on transfer and boundary crossing,* London: Pergamon.

Turner, B. (1972) 'Community colleges: Cambridgeshire', *Education & Training,* 14: 118–20.

US Department of Education (no date) *NCLB.* Washington DC: US Department of Education. Online. Available: www.ed.gov/nclb/landing.jhtml?src=ln (accessed 8 April 2010).

W.K. Kellogg Foundation (2004) *Logic model development guide,* Battle Creek, MI: W.K. Kellogg Foundation.

Warren, M. R. (2005) 'Communities and schools: A new view of urban education reform', *Harvard Educational Review,* 75: 133–73.

Warren, M. R. and Hong, S. (2009) 'More than services: Community organising and community schools', in Deslandes, R. (Ed.) *International perspectives on contexts, communities and evaluated innovative practices: Family-school-community partnerships,* London: Routledge.

Watts, J. (1974) *The Countesthorpe experience : The first five years,* London: Allen and Unwin.

Weikart, D., Bond, J. and McNeil, J. (1978) *The Ypsilanti Perry Preschool Project: Preschool years and longitudinal results through fourth grade. Monographs of the High/Scope Educational Research Foundation. Number 3,* Ypsilanti, MI: High/Scope Educational Research Foundation.

Weiss, C. H. (1995) 'Nothing as practical as a good theory: Exploring theory-based evaluation for comprehensive community initiatives for children and families', in Connell, J., Kubisch, A. C., Schorr, L. B. and Weiss, C. H. (Eds) *New approaches to evaluating community initiatives: Concepts, methods and contexts,* Washington DC: The Aspen Institute.

Whalen, S. (2002) *Report of the evaluation of the Polk Bros. Foundation's Full Service Schools Initiative. Executive summary,* Chicago, IL: Chapin Hall Center for Children at The University of Chicago for the Polk Bros Foundation.

Wilkin, A., Kinder, K., White, R., Atkinson, M. and Doherty, P. (2003a) *Towards the development of extended schools,* London: DfES.

Wilkin, A., White, R. and Kinder, K. (2003b) *Towards extended schools: A literature review,* London: DfES.

Wilkinson, R. and Pickett, K. (2009) *The spirit level: Why more equal societies almost always do better,* London: Penguin Books.

Index

CPSIA information can be obtained at www.ICGtesting.com
Printed in the USA
BVOW02s1436080813

327970BV00003B/64/P

9 780415 548755